MY PARENTS

*Memoirs of
New World Icelanders*

MY PARENTS

*Memoirs of
New World Icelanders*

Edited by Birna Bjarnadóttir
and Finnbogi Guðmundsson

University of Manitoba Press

University of Manitoba Press
Winnipeg, Manitoba R3T 2N2 Canada
www.umanitoba.ca/uofmpress
Printed in Canada on acid-free paper by Friesens.

Design: Relish Design Studio

Library and Archives Canada Cataloguing in Publication

      My parents : memoirs of New World Icelanders
/ Birna Bjarnadottir, primary editor ; Finnbogi Gudmundsson, co-editor.

Translation of: Foreldrar mínir.
ISBN 978-0-88755-699-9

      1. Icelanders--Canada--Biography. 2. Icelanders – United States
– Biography. 3. Iceland – Emigration and immigration – History.
4. Immigrants – Canada – Biography. 5. Immigrants – United States
– Biography. I. Bjarnadottir, Birna, 1961- II. Finnbogi Guðmundsson,
1924-

FC106.I3F6713 2007   971'.004396100922   C2007-901566-2

Publication of this book has been made possible by a grant from
The Icelandic Language and Literature Fund, Department of Icelandic
Language and Literature at the University of Manitoba.

University of Manitoba Press gratefully acknowledges the financial
support for its publication program provided by the Government of
Canada through the Book Publishing Industry Development Program
(BPIDP), the Canada Council for the Arts, the Manitoba Arts Council,
and the Manitoba Department of Culture, Heritage and Tourism.

CONTENTS

PREFACE

*I*n the year 1956, a collection of memoirs written by second-generation Icelanders in North America was published in Iceland, titled *Foreldrar mínir: Endurminningar nokkurra Íslendinga Vestan hafs* (Reykjavík: Minning). The editor of the book, Dr. Finnbogi Guðmundsson, had served as the first Chair of Icelandic in the University of Manitoba´s Department of Icelandic Language and Literature. He seized the opportunity at the time and asked a number of people to write a piece on their parents, resulting in a collection of fourteen essays. The personal subject was of paramount significance, the parents belonging to the generation of pioneers in the Icelandic settlements across North America. Many decades later, Dr. Finnbogi Guðmundsson contacted Dr. David Arnason, who, at the time, served as the Acting Head of the Icelandic Department, and myself, wondering if a selection of these memoirs should be published in English. The current publication speaks for itself, a selection of seven essays from the fourteen originally published in 1956, chosen by Dr. Finnbogi Guðmundsson himself. This selection is intended to give readers a representative sample of the different experiences of this generation of Icelandic pioneers throughout North America.

I would like to thank Dr. David Arnason, the former Acting Head of the Department of Icelandic Language and Literature, for being supportive of the translation of the selected essays, published in the current collection. I would also like to thank the translators, Árný Hjaltadóttir, Katelin Parson, and David Gislason. Pat Odegard and Kristin Sumner were no less indispensable as co-readers and proofreaders of the translations.

The essays honour the memory of the Icelandic pioneers in North America and their children, but all those interested in the emigration from Europe to the New World in the latter part of the nineteenth century might rejoice. The same could be said of those people hunting after original sources on Icelandic immigrants and their children in North America at the end of the nineteenth century and the beginning of the twentieth. As such, the nature of these memoirs is singular in the sense that the reader is invited straight into the heart of these people's lives. Along with the ties of European history, cultural heritage, and shared circumstances, one cannot escape the richness of the individual experience. Last, but not least, the present collection of memoirs casts light on the subject of translation. The adventurous task of translating one language to another is at work, not to mention the highly creative, far-reaching, and indispensable enterprise of translating cultures.

On the world's stage, the emigration from Europe to the New World, and the lives and fates of immigrants and their descendants, are an ever-growing subject of exploration and research. The history and culture of Icelandic immigrants in North America have also become a matter of widespread interest on both sides of the Atlantic.[1] At the time of the publication of the original collection of memoirs in 1956, a little more than 100 years had passed since the second wave of Icelandic settlement took place in America.[2] The emigration started in 1855

---

[1] For those interested in Icelandic North American history, genealogy, photographs, and publication, as well as in aricles on Icelandic settlers and their history, see Nelson Gerrard's *Saga Publications and Research* interactive Web site: <www.sagapublications.com>.

[2] Finnbogi Guðmundsson, "Formáli" [Preface], in *Foreldrar mínir,* 5. For those interested in the densely rich and far from exhausted subject of the first Icelandic settlement in America, see, for example, Gísli Sigurdsson's *The Medieval Icelandic Saga and Oral Tradition. A Discourse on Method,* trans. Nicholas Jones (Cambridge: Milman Perry Collection, 2004).

on a small scale and gained considerable momentum around 1870 and onwards when large groups of Icelanders left the country, leaving parts of it almost empty. Within two decades, emigration slowed down again and, at the turn of the twentieth century, had almost come to a halt.[3] According to a rough estimate, during the period from 1855 to 1900, around 20,000 Icelanders emigrated, or 20% to 25% of the total population.[4] Like many other European countries at the time, Iceland was providing the history of the world with one of its most spectacular chapters in emigration.

The first to leave Iceland were a few Mormons, heading for Utah in the years from 1855 to 1860. In 1863, a group of Icelanders sailed to Brazil and settled there. In 1870, a few Icelanders left for Wisconsin, and, in 1872, a few more left for North America, this time to settle in Canada. It was in 1873 that the first large group of Icelandic emigrants left Iceland, some to settle in Canada, others in the United States, and a few in Brazil. In 1874, a group of 365 Icelandic immigrants arrived in Québec, heading for Kinmount, Ontario. Left with little choice but to move on from there, and with the promise of land in Manitoba, the Icelanders arrived on the shores of Lake Winnipeg in October of 1875, the site that still is referred to as "New Iceland." A year later, the so-called "large group" of 1200 people left Iceland for Manitoba. In the fall of that same year, 1876, the newcomers from Iceland faced the hard impact of the smallpox epidemic. However, ridden by death and broken dreams in a place that, for many people, had been imagined as the promised land, the Icelandic immigrants started to manifest their sturdy aspiration for literary activities and publication,

---

[3] Guðmundsson "Formáli," 5.
[4] See Guðjón Arngrímsson´s *Nýja Ísland. Saga of the Journey to New Iceland,* trans. Robert Christie (Winnipeg: Turnstone Press, 1997), 27.

thereby introducing to the New World a specific art of mixing the colours of red and black; blood and ink; life and literature. The year of 1877 was when the printing press, ordered from the United States, arrived and when the Icelandic settlers published the first issue of the first Icelandic newspaper in North America, *Framfari* (the Icelandic word for "progress").[5]

The collection of essays speaks for itself in regards to the Icelandic cultural heritage and the role of that heritage in the survival of the settlers and the making of the Icelandic nineteenth-century settlements of North America. It should be noted, though, that the above-mentioned art, mixing the two colours of blood and ink, life and literature, is based on an underlying philosophy, originating from the Norse Olympus. In short, death is held in high regard, but never as something separate from life. Without the final stroke, death, life remains both incomplete and inaccessible. Even the father of the Norse Olympus, the god Óðinn, cannot see through life, resulting not only in his love for poetry, warriors, and wise women, but also in his striking intimacy with the world of the dead. A border-crossing character by nature, he travels continuously to the other side, not in order to forget about his shortcomings at home, or in a state of perpetual death wish, but to bring back fragments of wisdom and insight concerning life and the living. Running the risk of a crude simplification regarding the ethically charged subject of the land-claiming process in North America at the time, or regarding the way in which the Icelanders belonged first and foremost to the extensive group of Europeans in their aims to claim a piece of land, I should also note that their philosophy

---

[5] The printing press, arriving in the fresh wound of the smallpox epidemic, and the publication of *Framfari* are only two events in a long, far from finished story of the printing and publishing activities of Icelandic–Canadians. An example of an early start that has not come to a halt: in 1886, the Icelandic newspaper *Heimskringla* was founded and printed in Winnipeg. In 1888, another Icelandic newspaper, *Lögberg*, was founded in the same city. These two amalgamated in the year 1956. The paper is still being published, now biweekly, and is one of the oldest ethnic newspapers in Canada.

of life might have been shared more easily with the Aboriginal peoples than with the other European settlers. If poetic justice, the question remains: for whom?

The reader of these memoirs will not only sail down the Icelandic River. He or she will also travel to other settlements in both Canada and the United States. Apart from the essays evoking descriptions of life in the Gimli area, Riverton, and Winnipeg, descriptions of other Canadian settlements, such as those in Saskatchewan and Alberta, are as vivid. The American experience is no less present in the settlements of Wisconsin, North Dakota, and Argyle and Minneota in Minnesota. As Dr. Finnbogi Guðmundsson writes in his preface to the original publication, the collection could never have been a complete description of all Icelandic settlements in North America. However, he does express the view that the examples might give the reader some idea of the life of the Icelandic pioneers.[6] The same wish is expressed about the current selection of essays.

Around fifty years ago, the editor of the original collection may have been right in reminding the reader of the realities separating him or her from the people who emigrated from Iceland in the latter part of the nineteenth century. The gap may have widened. The two continents are still an ocean apart. However, to cross the Atlantic Ocean on a ship, never to return (as was often the case), arriving in a foreign country with little more than a bountiful gift for fate to play with is different from travelling overnight, reaching the other side more or less intact, equipped, in a case of emergency, with a couple of electronic devices and bag of organic snacks. Likewise, I am tempted to remind the reader of the manifold reasons for the emigration. The reasons can, indeed, be as many as those who left.[7] No

---

[6] See Guðmunsson's "Formáli," 6.
[7] Ibid., 5.

wonder, then, that one experiences the dizzying effect of the subject and one's own shortcomings when trying to grasp, in full, the lives and fates of the New World Icelanders. "No one," writes Finnbogi Guðmundsson, "can describe in a sufficient manner the anguish experienced by the Icelanders who emigrated, this experience that lasted from the moment someone decided to leave until the same person was buried in a North American prairie soil."[8] As the reader of the book will discover, in addition to the countless and far from homogeneous feelings and points of view, the "anguish" experienced is of several kinds among the individuals in question.

It may be the right time, again, to listen to a few voices within the group of Icelandic immigrants. The close encounter with the richness of each and every individual experience also serves as a reminder of the vast cultural change that took place in the nineteenth century when the forceful wave of European immigrants landed on the shores of North America. These individuals did not necessarily depart from their familiar lives in order to be placed once and for all in a segregated category, labelled "the immigrant." Apart from various decisive—and not yet fully explored and researched—factors on both sides of the Atlantic, the experience of these individuals is far from one-sided. If anything, their experience is sufficiently described as "explosive." When arriving on a foreign shore, the immigrant cannot help but carry a few distinctive seeds of cultural heritage. As well, the immigrant might be the most accurate yardstick there is for measuring a few essential dimensions of the human condition itself, or how it feels to belong to humanity.[9]

---

[8] Ibid.

[9] Franz Kafka's *Amerika: The Man Who Disappeared,* trans. Michael Hofmann (New York: New Directions, 2004), might be a source to explore for those interested in the subject. The unfinished novel, published after Kafka's death, is set in America at the beginning of the twentieth century. Kafka, who never crossed the Atlantic Ocean himself but scarcely hit a false note in his exhaustingly perceptive travels in the land of human existence, allows his protagonist, the young Karl Rossman, to explore and experience—in a spell of faith—the ups and downs of the New World.

Stephan G. Stephansson, the poet, philosopher, social prophet, and farmer, one of the Icelandic pioneers written about in this book by his daughter Rósa Benediktsson, was no stranger to the immigrant condition. It was Stephansson who wrote in a poem: "I have acquired somehow / no fatherland."[10] Regardless of ethnic origins and the time in history, immigrants worldwide would relate instantly to this expression. However, the vast impact of Stephansson's individual experience is no less evident in all his work, writings, and poems, reaching far beyond the condition of an immigrant, as such. In the runes of his life and legacy, one perceives that the challenges of the immigrant condition cannot easily be separated from the task of being human.[11] The undeniable vulnerability of the Icelandic immigrants, combined with the extraordinary capacity to survive, again and again, a seemingly hopeless situation, therefore, does not reveal only the ancient, Icelandic mindset (as we would like to believe), but also the outlines of human existence. "We live in succession, in division, in parts, in particles," wrote Emerson, Stephansson's predecessor in the ranks of North American philosophers and social prophets, and one of his greatest sources of inspiration.[12] Few statements apply more acutely to the life and fate of an immigrant. But Emerson may not have been referring to one group of people in particular.

---

[10] Stephan G. Stephansson, "The Exile," in *Stephan G. Stephansson:. Selected Prose and Poetry*, ed. and trans. Kristjana Gunnars (Alberta: Red Deer College Press, 1988), 75.

[11] Stefan M. Jonasson has written a beautiful piece on Stephan G. Stephansson's far-reaching talents, gifts, and humanity. See Jonasson's "Out in the Open Air. The Liberating Legacy of Stephan G. Stephansson," *The Icelandic Canadian* 58, 2 (2003): 51–63. Haraldur Bessason, former Chair of the Department of Icelandic Language and Literature, is no less perceptive of Stephansson's profound contribution in his piece, "Where the Limitations of Language and Geography Cease to Exist," *The Icelandic Canadian* 24, 4 (1967): 47–53, 72–76.

[12] Ralph Waldo Emerson, "The Over-Soul," in *Ralph Waldo Emerson*, ed. Richard Poirier (Oxford and New York: Oxford University Press, 1990), 153. In his biography on Stephan G. Stephansson, in particular in the first volume, *Landneminn mikli*, Viðar Hreinsson discusses the Emerson-Stephansson relation, emphasizing the profound impact of Emerson's writings on Stephansson's view of life and work ethic (Reykjavík: Bjartur, 2002).

This brings me to my final note, the subject of translation. The essays in the collection were originally written in Icelandic. When published in Iceland in 1956, there was, nevertheless, a translation taking place, not between one language and another, but between cultures. Around the middle of the twentieth century, Icelanders were poorly informed of the lives and fates of Icelandic immigrants and their descendants in North America. In the current collection of the seven selected essays, there is a more obvious act of translation taking place between one language and another. Only one of the original essays has been previously translated and published in English: the piece on Stephan G. Stephansson and his wife Helga Jónsdóttir, written by their daughter Rósa Benediktsson.[13] However, the subject of translating cultures is no less dense, for the Icelanders who left Iceland in the latter part of the nineteenth century have been prolific in providing two continents with the fruit of their lives and fates, translating, on both sides, one culture to another. Meanwhile, all the policies, often designed in high places, emphasizing the importance of embracing cultural diversity and tolerance towards foreign seeds, and distributed through governmental channels in the form of flawlessly written reports, tend to circulate above and below the lifeline of the people in question.

Judging from their continuous art in mixing the two colours, blood and ink, life and literature, Icelandic-Canadians are as sturdy as ever. One could foresee the following memoir, in a future collection, written by an Icelandic-Canadian who initially aspired to writing and eventually became a poet on the big screen: Guy Maddin. We are on Ellice Avenue in Winnipeg in the latter

---

[13] The piece was translated by Nina Campbell and published in Joanne White's *Stephan's Daughter. The Story of Rosa Siglaug Benediktson* (Calgary: Benson Ranch, 2003).

part of the twentieth century, witnessing the highly creative, far-reaching, and indispensable enterprise of translating cultures:

> As a hedge against catatonic depression, for years I gave all the print reviews to my Gramma, who would translate them out loud into Icelandic to her big brother Hjalmar, who in turn would promptly translate them sentence by sentence, with a shrill dental whistle, right back into his own archaic approximation of English, while I listened in a cold sweat.
>
> By the time my review went through this two-stage process, it no longer frightened me, having acquired the flavours of a bowdlerized Nordic folktale. Most of the cruelties were recouched in quaint hearthside metaphors with more charm than stomps. Even better, the not infrequent praise warbled out in the singsong falsetto peculiar to Icelandic typically depicted me as a mighty storytelling slayer of Hollywood ogres, a fair-haired god with wisdoms infinite, or some kind of mischievous lava sprite—all good things!
>
> I never suspected generous mistranslation, but when these two handy ancestors of mine recently climbed up to Valhalla, I hauled out my clippings to reread the encomia. Without fail, I was shocked at the sorry level of writing in the original English text, film journalism as sloppily hammered together and painted as a kid's clubhouse—no grace of line, no awareness of harmony, no evidence of an eye. And this was the positive press! Really! [14]

---

[14] Guy Maddin, *From the Atelier Tovar: Selected Writings* (Toronto: Coach House Books, 2003), 91.

The New World is ferried over to the sentiment of the old country, Iceland, only to be revisited with all strings attached, embodied by the Norse Olympus itself. There is a singular air to this adventure, as if one is entering a world of its own, separated from everything and everyone, an island on Ellice Avenue, surrounded by the oceanic continent of North America. Therein lies its beauty. For this household scene is, in fact, an arrow, shot through the heart of a culture defined as North American. The Icelandic pioneers' households across the new countries were no different, more or less singular in the art of belonging.

—*Birna Bjarnadóttir*

MY PARENTS

*Memoirs of
New World Icelanders*

ÓLAFUR G. JOHNSON &
SIGÞRÚÐUR GUÐBRANDSDÓTTIR

❖

BY MRS. SIGURLÍNA BACKMAN,
WINNIPEG, MANITOBA

"Life was not all play, at least not for my parents ..."

*M*any years ago when I was working as a nurse in Chicago, an old woman who had hurt her knee was brought into my ward. While I was caring for her I found out that she was Icelandic and her name was Júlíana Þórðarson, the wife of Hjörtur, an electrical engineer. I told her that I was also Icelandic and that cheered her up. We talked and she began to recall memories from home. She lay with her eyes closed and spoke as if she was talking to herself. "There is one thing that stands out so clearly in my mind while I was still in Iceland," she said. "There was a seventeen-year-old girl, very beautiful and just married, who was on her way to America. She wept so bitterly when she said goodbye to her mother." After a short time she continued. "Her name was Sigþrúður and her mother was Ástríður."

"What was her husband's name?" I asked.

"His name was Ólafur, a minister's son and very handsome."

"I know the couple," I said. "They are my parents."

My father Ólafur Johnson was the son of Rev. Guðmundur Johnson at Arnarbæli by the Ölfus River and Guðrún Pétursdóttir (Hjaltested). My mother's name was Sigþrúður and she was the daughter of Guðbrandur and Ástríður at Hákot on Álftanes.

I tried at times to find out why my parents moved from Iceland, this land that everyone was talking, reading, and singing about. My father's family was well off and he had received an above-average education. The longing to see the world was probably strong because when he was about twenty he went with some of his friends to America and stayed in Milwaukee for two years. However, he went home when he received news of his father's death. He had drowned in the Ölfus River on his way home from a baptism. Going back home was hard. Not only had he lost his father but also his home and the place where he grew up. A new minister had moved to Arnarbæli, and his mother and siblings had moved to Reykjavík.

After a few months at home he again began to think about moving to America. His sister Ingibjörg was moving to America and she insisted that he accompany her. My father did not reject this idea because he had liked living in America and therefore had some idea about what life was like there. At the time, he was just about to marry and the decision was made to leave after the wedding. In their party were Ingibjörg, her fiancé Sigurður, my parents, and many others. This was in 1876 and the group arrived in Winnipeg in October. The trip ended sadly for Ingibjörg. Her fiancé Sigurður drowned in the Red River just before they landed in Winnipeg. He had fallen overboard in the dark of night and could not swim. Two weeks later Ingibjörg herself found the corpse where it had washed ashore. After the funeral the siblings went their separate ways. Ingibjörg stayed in Winnipeg and my parents went to Gimli.

They remembered the first winter quite well because that was when smallpox raged among the pioneers in Gimli. My parents had no children at the time and they did not come down with smallpox so they were able to lend their neighbours a helping hand and this they did willingly. They often mentioned the difficulties and the sorrow, as there were whole families that died of the disease. One home was so full of caskets that it was difficult to enter the house. One couple lost all seven of their children.

My parents only stayed that one winter in Gimli and then they moved to Winnipeg, where they lived for the next few years. They seldom mentioned that period of their lives. It was full of painful memories. They lost their first three children to diphtheria. My father's sister, Ingibjörg, had married Helgi Jónsson (the editor of the periodical *Leifur*) and had a son. She lost both of them in the same week and they were buried in the same grave.

Next they moved to North Dakota for a while and I know little about their lives during that time. A letter from my father's mother is still in existence where she points out to them that they could return home. My father also received a letter from his relative, President Jón Sigurðsson, who told him it was their duty to come home and live in their fatherland. I do believe that this situation was a dilemma for them because my mother's relatives were on the verge of sailing to America.

Then they moved to the Þingvalla settlement in Saskatchewan and settled there. A short time later, my mother's relatives arrived and settled close by. Ingibjörg, my father's sister, had already moved there. She had married a second time (Bjarni Westman) and they operated a store in Churchbridge. My parents lived in the Þingvalla settlement for twelve wonderful years, or so I have been told, surrounded by friends, acquaintances, and relatives. The settlers all faced similar conditions and they helped one another out. The settlement did not have a minister and my father was often asked to perform this duty. My father was very much involved with the social activities of the district and at most gatherings he delivered a speech or an original poem. My mother was known for her good advice and her willingness to help those who were sick. She often walked many miles to care for others.

It was probably difficult to leave the Þingvalla settlement and to move away from all their loved ones, but there was no other choice. The dry weather from lack of rain was destroying the farmland. More than half the settlers moved away and drove their animals with them. Many went west, but my parents went east and stopped in an English-speaking district close to Strathclair, Manitoba. I was six years old at the time and therefore I was beginning to become aware of what was going on around me.

This was a great change in our lives. There were fields here and lakes and large forests. For the young it was a dreamland. Our home stood in the middle of a clearing at the edge of a lake. In the lake were a few islands, majestic and forested, with places that provided an endless adventure for us children. We often went to the islands with our lunches and picked berries, which grew there in abundance.

Another thing that amazed us were the cornfields, which shone in the summer sun. We had never seen a crop like this before. Nevertheless, life was not all play, at least not for my parents. The family was large with ten children in all. Two of the oldest ones left home at a young age so my parents had little help initially. It must have been difficult for my mother to care for this large family. We all had home-knitted socks and underwear and even dresses that were crocheted. She worked and spun the wool from our own sheep.

We were a rambunctious group, in part because we were all healthy and were therefore full of energy. When Father sat in the evening and sang, it was as if a heavenly peace settled over the home. As soon as the lamp was lit, he took a book and read the Old Icelandic sagas aloud.

My father always did the most difficult work such as clearing new land. Once I was sent with his coffee to where he was working. I was always eager to go because it was enjoyable to sit and talk with him. He was always so funny and happy. It was an unusually hot day and Father was glad to sit down and wait when he saw me coming. "What, no sour whey?" he said. A moment later, he threw the coffee down and jumped up and ran as fast as he could to the lake. I ran after him, completely amazed. Could he be this angry because he didn't get a cold drink? I was more than a little surprised when he jumped into the water and dove under. He acted like a wild man, waving his arms and slapping himself. He happened to look at me where I stood dumbfounded on the bank and he let out a peal of laughter. "It was a darn anthill I was sitting on," he said.

My parents did well there. We produced many different products on our farm—mostly corn, but also butter, meat, and eggs. We often took large quantities of berries to town in the summer. But there were only six years of good fortune there because then our large house burned to the ground in January, along with all the furniture, clothes, and a decent Icelandic library. The yearning to live in an Icelandic district had always been strong, and in June we moved to the Marshland settlement, near where the town of Langruth is now situated.

My father bought land on the outskirts of the settlement. It was very grassy land and its boundaries seemed unlimited. Summer was almost over and there was no time to waste. There was a lot to do. A house and a barn had to be built, and hay had to be put up for the animals before winter set in. Everything worked out and the winter passed without much happening. Everyone who could help was called on to work outside, to look after the animals, to bring them water and clean the barn. There were now seven children at home; the oldest was a boy of fourteen and the youngest was two years old. The three oldest ones had moved away.

There had been little opportunity to go to school in our previous location because it was so far to travel and the teacher was worn out. The following summer we were fortunate that J. Magnús Bjarnason was hired. He was a renowned elementary schoolteacher and a writer.[1] People soon realized that this man had many other talents. I am not going to describe him here, as it is sufficient to say that he impressed us all. He instructed us and instilled in us many principles with his unique and gentle

---

[1] Jóhann Magnús Bjarnason (1865–1945) was one of the leading writers among Icelandic immigrants in North America. He wrote the novel *Brazilíufararnir* (Winnipeg: Lögberg, 1905–1908), the novel *Eiríkur Hansson* (Akureyri: Oddur Björnsson, 1899–1903), numerous short stories and poems. See also Bjarnason's collection of short stories, *Errand Boy in the Mooseland Hills*, trans. Borga Jakobson (Halifax: Formac Publishing Company Limited, 2001). (Ed.)

but serious manner. Magnús and my father became friends from the start. They sat together and talked for long periods of time. Often one would hear them discussing poetry or telling stories. "It is so much fun to tell your father a story," Magnús said to me, "he is always so attentive." On his birthday, May 24, Magnús and his wife Guðrún came for a visit. It was such a joyous occasion and Magnús told me many years later that those had been the most enjoyable days during his stay in Marshland. Their friendship lasted throughout their lives. I often heard Magnús recite a poem that my father had composed for him, after he (Magnús) had moved to the west coast. I still remember three verses from one of the poems, which follow:

Það mér valinn þykir dvalar staður,
sem báran væg ei brýtur land,
en buldrar hæg við fjörusand.

Á þessum bletti þú munt settur vera,
þar sem björkin bein og há
byrgir mörk við kalda lá.

Það veit Drottinn, þú átt gott að lifa
og horfa á sjóinn hamast þar
og hlusta á skógar raddirnar.

It's my belief we've chosen well a place to dwell,
where surly ocean breakers cannot reach,
but gentle waves caress the sandy beach.

On these few acres you will make your home,
where the birches straight you see,
frame the forest by the sea.

> God has understood, life will be good,
> watching as each new wave rejoices,
> hearing the sound of forest voices.[2]

The second year in our new home began promisingly enough, as a great many things had been achieved. Now we could catch our breath and wait for the next challenge. But this sense of well-being came to a sudden end.

For the second time, we experienced an enormous loss by fire. This time, it was the barn and some of the animals. I remember this event well. We were beside ourselves with panic as we ran outside. The fire was so great that nothing could be done. The loud crashing noises were terrible but to hear the screams of the poor animals in the barn was the worst. Through all this noise, we heard Mother call: "Hurry, boys, go after your father. He has gone into the barn and the door slammed shut." The boys were quick to go after Father and led him out. He walked doubled over and exhausted toward the house and sat down on a small hill and cried. Worst of all was to see my father so completely shattered. But before too long he was back to his happy self. My mother had an enchanting way of comforting him during difficult times like these. They did not dwell on this situation for long and another barn was soon built, although smaller than the first one.

Social life flourished in the district, gatherings were held frequently, and an Icelandic library was established. My parents were content in this environment and it is safe to say that their farm did well.

> Hrokkið hafa árin, hratt með tímans straum,
> ég lít í gegnum tárin, og skoða liðinn draum.

---

[2] All verses, unless otherwise attributed, are translated by David Gislason.

How rapidly time passes, relentless as a stream.
Through my tears I reminisce, tending a bygone dream.

To me it seems like yesterday that we were all together on that farm not far from Langruth. I look back and I see it all so clearly in my mind—our home, on the western edge of the old settlement, where the view was breathtaking, where the blood-red lilies, as if they were smiling at the sun, opened their arms over the land. It was a beautiful scene and especially so in the evenings, when the rays from the setting sun passed over the faraway mountaintops [Riding Mountain] and turned the western sky into a blazing spectacle.

I always felt that our house looked so lonely because there weren't any trees right around it. Still, it was the place that was closest to our hearts. The sky was so blue and the air so fresh. There we played, laughed, and cried together. We enjoyed life especially during spring because then the weather was often so beautiful. The air was filled with chirping and beautiful bird songs. All of nature burned with the expectation of love. It would be fun if one could go back for one mild spring day to dance around with the doves and play with the lambs. I cannot say much good about the winter because there was not much shelter around the house and there was so much snow. The snowdrifts towered over everything. Sometimes we went sledding off the haystacks because those were the only hills around. I also remember the cold weather and the blizzards that could appear all of a sudden.

I will never forget how afraid we were one time when one of the boys was on his way home from town on a cold winter evening. It was pitch-black outside and the drifting snow made it impossible to see anything. My father paced the floor back and forth because he was so worried, but Mother was not agitated. She sat calmly by her spinning wheel and didn't say much, except once in a while she said to Father, "Sit down, my dear, pacing back and forth doesn't help at all." She said this mainly to settle him down and to reassure him. She was always so strong and calm in those situations. On the other hand, it was the little things that irritated her—for instance, when her thimble disappeared—whereas my father was never bothered by these small incidents.

Our house was always full of life. We were never bored because there were so many of us children, and there was always so much to do. In the mornings we had to rush, first to finish milking because we had many cows, and then to be on time for school, which was five kilometres away from home. This busy routine was good for us, but best of all was to come home after school to have coffee and Icelandic pancakes or *kleinur*.[3] Here we were cared for, here we had warmth, and here was our *mother*. It was no wonder that our world revolved around her because she

> þjónaði, þvoði og þurrkaði tárin,
> bakaði, bætti og batt um sárin.

> watched and washed and wiped our tears,
> cooked and clothed and calmed our fears.

Mother cared about everything, big and small. There was never a hole too small in a sock that it wasn't mended by morning.

Although occasionally the hustle and bustle seemed a bit much, there was another side to our life out in the country and that was the peaceful evenings when my father sang and recited ballads. I was always aware of being filled with peace and happiness when I listened to him. Everyone admired his ability to sing.

---

[3] Kleinur are similar to doughnuts. (Trans.)

I have many images of my parents and the following one is the most memorable.

In the early years my mother worked hard out in the garden, which was a short distance from the house, and it was something that she never totally gave up because gardening made her feel good. She would often go out for a while in the evening. One evening she went out to the garden. Everything was still but thunder in the distance indicated that a change was imminent. Mother didn't let it bother her, even though the sky became overcast and the thunder grew louder. As the evening passed and she didn't come home, my father became so worried that he finally went out to call her. When he saw the fury of the impending storm, he thought it would be too late for Mother to get out of its way and so he ran to where she knelt, still busy with her work. He crouched down beside her to be close to her so that the same fate might befall both of them.

My parents were very close even though they were quite unlike each other in many ways. Father was always busy with poetry. He was skilled in verse making and composed many beautiful poems. This is the last verse he composed before he died:

Heyrðu Jesú, ó heyrðu mig,
hjálpaðu mér að lofa þig,
veittu mér frið í vöku og blund,
og vertu hjá mér á dauða stund.

Hear me Jesus, O hear my song,
help me to sing your praises long.
Grant me your peace as I wake or sleep,
in my dying hour, a vigil keep.

Often, reciting poetry was the last thing he did at night and the first thing he did in the morning. He was an industrious and hard-working man, but was always a dreamer at heart. He was also happy, modest, and generous, and was always mild-mannered and gentle, both with us children and my mother. We were so very important to him and I don't remember that he ever laid a hand on us children. Perhaps that was because we were never naughty or disrespectful when he was around. We were especially well-behaved and didn't dare to move an inch during family prayers. He did not let anything distract him from this ritual, even when a non-Icelander came over during the Icelandic reading.

Mother showed tremendous courage. She was never afraid of anything, she was exceptionally loyal, and she didn't tolerate any unkind words about anyone. She was tall, had a good figure, and was quick-thinking and skilled with her hands. My mother's works were many and so remarkable that words can't describe them. Unfortunately, in her old age, she suffered twice from broken bones and both times she was bedridden for a long time. She never lost her spirit and never once did anyone hear her complain. Those who knew her when she was young said that she had been very beautiful. Her children and everyone who loved her thought she was beautiful until the end. Her beauty was, of course, different now, more, if you like, of a spiritual nature. Peace and happiness shone from her.

My parents' golden wedding anniversary was celebrated in Langruth. Family and friends came from all over to the celebration. This was the only time when all of us, siblings and parents, were together. But this is often the case with big families in large countries.

I will never forget when my parents entered the hall. They both looked so dignified, as always, and I cannot describe how I felt as I watched them.

Shortly after that, my parents moved to Winnipeg and lived peacefully with my sister for the rest of their lives. My mother died in 1943 at the age of eighty-five and my father in 1949 at the age of ninety-seven. They had been married for sixty-seven years.

—*Translated by Árný Hjaltadóttir*

STEPHAN G. STEPHANSSON & HELGA JÓNSDÓTTIR

❖

BY RÓSA BENEDIKTSSON

*M*y father was Stephan Guðmundsson, son of Guðmundur Stefánsson and his wife Guðbjörg Hannesdóttir. My mother was Helga Jónsdóttir, daughter of Jón Jónsson and his wife Sigurbjörg Guðmundsdóttir. All these people moved to America together in the year 1873, from Bárðardal in Suður-Þingeyrarsýsla, in the north of Iceland.

I think my first memory of my father was in connection with "Ash Day," and I was very young then. Having heard that people had to bear ashes on that day, I put some ashes in my father's shoes. I remember that he spoke seriously to me and expressed his disapproval, which still sticks in my memory.

The picture becomes clearer and I visualize a rather short and slender man, stooped at the shoulders and showing signs of having worked hard over the years. His face was rough-hewn and he had a high forehead. His hair was dark, with grey streaks.

When he was eighteen he had lost a lot of his hair. He had a reddish moustache but it was his eyes that were the most memorable. They were blue, sharp, and deep-set, and when he grinned, they seemed to twinkle. He had a serious appearance, was never boisterous, but when spoken to, he always responded in the same agreeable manner, no matter what the circumstances, because of his unusual composure. He went quietly about his work, and sometimes composed his poetry in low tones.

My mother was quite short in stature, somewhat stout as I remember her first, with light-coloured eyebrows and lashes. She was rather more excitable, but easygoing, and she moved quickly. A more selfless person would be difficult to find. She greatly enjoyed instrumental music and song, had a pleasant voice, and was very knowledgeable and always humming tunes while she worked.

My parents and their parents on both sides moved from Iceland in 1873 to Wisconsin in the USA. They were married there in 1878, and two sons, Baldur and Guðmundur, were born. In 1880 they moved to the Gardar District in North Dakota and became settlers there. All the relatives moved with them, including both parents of my mother and father, along with Jón, my maternal uncle, and Sigurlaug Einara, my paternal aunt. There were no other siblings. Their family's homestead land was near the village of Gardar, close to the land of my Afi [grandfather] Jón, where his descendants live to this day. It was there that my brothers Jakob and Jón were born. My brother Jón and Afi Guðmundur died and were buried there.

In the early spring of 1889, several families in the Icelandic community in North Dakota pulled up stakes again to become settlers in Canada. The trip was to take them to the province of Alberta, the second province from the west coast in this vast land.

My parents went in that group with my three brothers, Amma Guðbjörg and Sigurlaug, my father's sister, and her family. Their destination was Calgary, and, since it was the last stop on the railway at the time, everyone got out there. My parents had come with all their household goods and a team of oxen. The promised land was still a long way off so it was necessary to keep going forward, travelling with heavily laden wagons pulled by cattle. The women and children remained for a time in Calgary. My mother and paternal aunt made good use of their time by working as laundresses for the so-called "gentlewomen" of the town. My father and several men from his district equipped themselves to travel on and set off with their ox team to explore the countryside. It was decided to travel in a northerly direction for some 130 kilometres where the town of Innisfail now stands, and then turn west. The majestic Rocky Mountains were always visible to the west, standing almost like guardians. The mountains likely played a role in determining the direction the explorers took by luring them on westward. They crossed the swift-flowing Red Deer River and continued onward past fertile agricultural land until they reached the banks of the Medicine River. There they found a place to settle amid high hills. They selected a site for a house that has remained to this day on a hill to the east of the river. The Rocky Mountains loomed in the west more than 160 kilometres away and the countryside could have reminded them of their distant fatherland, Iceland. They had now travelled over 1600 kilometres from the town of Gardar and there was much work to do, building homes and getting down to the business of settling on the land.

Many people may ask, "Why did they leave the fertile land of the Red River Valley and what was there to attract them to this wilderness?" There could have been many reasons. The unsettled land tempted them and encouraged them to set up shelter there and provide for themselves. There was no lack of the steadfastness, vigour, or daring that were needed. I remember that my mother declared that each new settlement made them younger. Nevertheless, it must have been painful to leave her aged parents, whom she never saw again, and certainly my father must have missed the many firm friends he left behind. Those bonds of friendship were never completely severed, as evidenced by the correspondence that continued between my father and his friends all their lives. Perhaps in this isolation my father was able to find himself and devote himself more to his interests. One thing is certain: by broadening his horizons he came under influences that have been reflected in the poems that we now enjoy. Certainly, the ever-changing landscape in Alberta reminded him of Iceland. He states in his poem "West to the New Settlement": "After I set off to roam, I feel I have come home," etc.

Later that summer, my father returned to Calgary to get the family. Nothing is said of the trip until they come to the Red Deer River. The wagon was heavily laden with household goods and my mother and three brothers sat on the top. My father walked ahead of the oxen and led them across the river. The Red Deer River often floods due to snow melt in the summer heat and is swift with a strong current as the stream comes down from the Rocky Mountains. When Father led the oxen to the middle of the river, the current was so strong that he momentarily lost his footing. He looked over his shoulder and my mother smiled at him and he then regained his balance. They reached the shore without further incident. In the poem "Forgotten Travelling Obstacles" this incident in their life was immortalized in the last two verses:

His wife looked at him then
trusting with a smile on her lips
between the children, on the edge of the seat
Since then he always believed
that her smile in particular was all
that triumph depended on, that kept
everything afloat.

I remember my mother said, "I was never afraid then," notwithstanding that in later years she was often apprehensive if her loved ones were delayed for some reason.

Then my family moved into the new home, a log cabin, and then, on a wonderful fall day, October 6 [1889], my twin sisters were born. They were like night and day. The older one was dark-haired and named Stephany Guðbjörg; the other one was blonde and was named Jony Sigurbjörg. In the year 1893, a son was born, named Gestur Cecil, in honour of the poet Gestur Pálsson and Cecelia the midwife. Finally, in 1900, I, the last-born baby of the family, was born and named Siglaug Rósa. My father thought that the "ur" in the name Sigurlaug was unnecessary, so I am sure that I am the only woman to have that name. My second name was my great-grandmother's name.

Later that summer, my father's sister had moved with her family to the north of the district, and settled near our home, but on the other side of the river. My Amma came with her, and she moved to my parents' home, where she lived until she died. Before I proceed further, I would like to say a few words about them. My father's sister Sigurlaug, or "Tanta" as we called her—a term from the Norwegian district in Wisconsin—was different in appearance from my father. She had brown eyes and smooth black hair, which was never out of place. She was intelligent, entertaining, and extremely calm, a true heroine in all of life's tribulations. I was never aware that she had any poetic gifts. She worked as a midwife for most of her life. She and my father did not visit each other much, though they lived so close. It was enough for them to know they were nearby. Both were homebodies and not given to travel. My greatest joy was to visit my namesake Tanta the midwife.

My Amma had two rooms for her use. There she sat with her fine handwork and read books. Sometimes my sisters read aloud for her, because she taught them Icelandic. It was my bad luck to be the youngest and miss out on many such good things. She read English, which of course she taught herself, crocheted the finest lace, and spun and knitted with great skill for as long as she remained in good health. She also braided sedge and made hats for the boys out of hemp. She had a deep love for her only son. He had been born with a caul on his head, whether that superstition meant anything or not. My mother did her best to see that Amma was comfortable and she lived to a ripe old age. My father then wrote a poem, which goes:

> in thanks, with its shining wreath of love
> here rests your weary mothering heart.

The first years of pioneering must have been hard and busy. For two summers, my father went to work as a surveyor in the northern part of the province with a group of men. I think that the "outlaw" life agreed with him. I heard him mention that. My mother remained at home with her children and Amma. One summer, when my father was away, a prairie fire came roaring out of the west. The fire jumped across the river and headed straight for our house. The people in the house were prepared to flee, but at the foot of the hill the soil was wet, which killed the fire and everything was saved.

The first schoolhouse in the district was built on the hill just east of our house. In 1893 the men in the district built it from logs. It was named Hóla School and the name still remains in that district. In order for as many children as possible to attend the school, those who lived quite a distance away stayed at my parents' home. Our home also became an obvious place for the teacher to live as it was so close to the school, and many of them stayed there. The school was used as a meeting hall and served as the centre of social life in the district.

There were many good times at our farm. The first Icelandic Day celebrations were held on the land there and the Icelandic flag was hoisted on a high hill northeast of the homesite. The hill has been known as "Flag Hill" since then. I never heard my father call his farm by name but the hills were given names: "Langás" [Long Ridge] was the ridge east of the farm and below that was "Mosamyri" [Mossy Moorland]. North of that was "Fagrabrekka" [Beautiful Slope] or "Fagrihöll" [Beautiful Hill], and from there was a view far and wide. My father nicknamed the Medicine River "Huld" [Secret]. The Indians had named it for their greatest magician, the "Medicine Man." I do not know if any magic power was concealed in its calm mean derings but it must have charmed my father, for he wrote in his poem "The River": "T'would be a joy to live beside you ever and unending"—and so it came to pass.

As circumstances permitted, the house was improved and enlarged until it took on its present form, which is how I first remember it. Most of it was built of logs and clad inside and out. First there was the hall or "Big House," as it was always called. It was a large room and had an upstairs. My father's study was west of that with bay windows facing south and two facing west. It was always called the *kompa* [cubbyhole]. In the north part of the house, there was a small room partitioned off, which was my parents' bedroom. Then there was a kitchen in the east part of the main house and a pantry just off it. We girls slept in the bedroom that was on the south side. The boys slept upstairs and our grandmother had the use of two rooms on the north side of the house. On the south side, there was an attic, while the door on the big house faced south, with a balcony over it. This is what our house was like. We always felt it was a warm and comfortable fortress against the storms of life.

My mother was always first to rise in the morning and always brought my father and all the members of the household coffee in bed. My brothers and sisters helped with the household chores and were not often away from home. My father looked after the animals and was a true animal lover. He worked at haying and cutting grain, especially stacking the bales. He never ground the wheat, as my mother and sisters did that. In the winter my father wrote letters and other correspondence in the mornings, and in the afternoon he would go straight to his study to read and write and compose. Each moment was put to good use. I remember well on winter nights, sitting in a corner in the twilight, listening to him reciting his poems. In the middle of the room was a large, round fireplace, which burned brightly. I remember often seeing him coming in from the barn in the cold weather, in a great hurry to write down some lines before they were lost. When my father was preparing his poems for printing, he was extremely busy and often stayed awake well into the night. Then my mother would get up at midnight and make him some coffee.

There is one unforgettable event that took place in my younger years. My father felt strongly that the school was deficient, that all students were cast in the same mould there and individuality stifled. "Here is an unhealthy atmosphere," he stated in his poem "Children's School." But it turned out that I was sent to school. I was rather timid and did not know a word of English. My father took me by the hand and led me to the school and entrusted me to the care of the schoolteacher. I will never forget that walk. I was filled with confidence as he guided me down the path by the river.

We often had visitors. Neighbours who lived along the riverbank made it a habit to come by and chat for a while and have a cup of coffee, and they often brought the mail from town. Everyone knew how important it was for my father to get his mail. I remember my father calling, "Start making coffee, Helga, your Guðmundur has arrived."

The very first years we were there, we had two visitors from Winnipeg, B.L. Baldwinson and another guest. Our house was very small, so a canvas tent was put over a wagon box and they slept there that night. It was summertime and that was quite acceptable. When the visitors were getting ready to leave, Baldwin asked, "What do I owe you for the favour?" and my mother replied: "Oh, bless you, don't mention it, you had nothing but porridge." He then replied, "Do you think that I want to eat up all your porridge, woman!" My mother laughed at that incident.

It sometimes happened that people stayed with my parents if their circumstances were temporarily difficult. I remember hearing that in North Dakota the mother of electrical engineer Hjörtur Þórðarson stayed with them one winter. She was a widow with two young sons and life was tough for them. She had only one cow and made thick soup by adding grain to the milk and cooking it. Hjörtur was considered introverted and dreamy, my mother said. One day, when he was near my mother's stove, one of the lids on it broke. Hjörtur was so upset that my father said to him, "Oh, bless you, don't be sorry about this. Maybe you can make it up to Helga for the broken lid some time." Many years later he richly rewarded them. He sent my father a large collection of books and gifts of money to both of them. I said he was making up for the broken lid.

There are many happy memories of the many travellers who visited my father, among them several ministers and professors, some straight from Iceland. My father relished becoming acquainted with them and many discussions were held on everything from philosophy to the newest farming methods.

Sveinbjörn Sveinbjörnsson, the composer, came twice, and it was most enjoyable to watch him compose a tune to my father's poem "Hugsað Heim" ["Home Thoughts"] on our old organ. He was like a bird on a branch, the old man, as he flew from the organ to the table to write down the notes. Our mother's brother Jón, whom we always called "Unkel," came three times from North Dakota to visit us. The Rev. Rögnvaldur Pétursson came often. I remember that the first time that both and he and his wife came, the Stampede was being held at Benalto and my father wanted them to see that activity so much that he went with them for the first and only time. There was a heavy rainfall and I recall the trip being much more uncomfortable than it had promised to be, when we were going home.

My father was hardly ever away from home. In the early years it was customary to have community parties at holiday times like Christmas and New Year's Day. All the family would attend and stay all night. Sometimes we went east over the hill for quite a distance, as far as fifteen or twenty kilometres. One time my father went home on foot early in the morning, ahead of the other people, to heat the house and feed the animals.

Sometimes friends came over with the intention that "we will have a feast" and they did not come empty-handed. Generally, these were Auðna-Bjarni [Bjarni from the Wilderness], Strandar Jón [Jón from Geiteyjarstrond], Viðimýrar Siggi [Siggi from Viðimýri], Kristinn [brother-in-law], and others who had joined the group. Then Icelandic songs were sung with gusto until the first rosy rays of dawn appeared. My father was no singer, but if he had a few under his belt, he would begin by singing the English hymn "In the Sweet By and By."

There were often intense disputes about the First World War. I remember that my father said that there would never be peace in Europe until all the countries would unite in the "United Nations of Europe," with a common government, and, in fact, many people are now of this opinion. My father was always liberal in his ideas, and his liberal views grew stronger as he aged. He had such faith in mankind, and that, in the course of time, it would be possible to educate the common people so that they could live in peace and harmony and everyone would have all they needed, provided the system under which people lived was just. At other times, there were arguments about religion. I remember that one of his old friends was rather hard on Catholic views. My father was explaining their side. In all discussions I felt he was a "champion of the underdog." I heard him say of the spiritualists that "This is something that we still do not understand, but maybe, when it is possible to assert that 'thoughts are things,' we can understand it better."

My mother enjoyed telling us this story of the Dakota years. It was a matter of course for everyone in the United States to attend the 4th of July celebrations. The whole family went by ox team, and on one occasion when they neared a stream on the way, the oxen took control away from Grandpa, waded into the water, and upset the wagon, and everyone's best clothes were soaked. Someone had forgotten to water the oxen that morning. They did not let this stop them but went instead to a friend's house, dried their clothes, and continued on as if nothing had happened.

When my father was able to use his study and things were quieter, and he had help with the farm, he wrote more poetry. By then he had travelled widely and come under a wide range of influences. He kept all this in his mind, as he was endowed with an exceptional memory of everything he had read or seen. It may have helped that he had not attended school. Often, when something came up that we did not understand, the call went out: "Let's ask Pabbi," and he solved our problems quickly and well. Even today, when I have a problem, I ask Pabbi. I find the solutions and comfort in his poems.

If my mother was downhearted, my father used to tell her, "Don't let it get to you. It will all turn out somehow." But it was in times of trouble that my parents showed their greatest strength of character. It was a tragic blow for the household when my brother Gestur was struck by lightning. Those were sad days but my father, with his usual steadfastness, had a friend build a casket for him, and then he wrote a eulogy in Gestur's memory, which was read at the funeral. The whole family agreed with him when he wrote:

> Among the angelic host in joy and gladness
> Gestur will be my guest—and nowhere else.

At the instigation of his many friends, my father sometimes travelled on long trips, which gave him much pleasure and added variety to his life. In 1908 his first long trip took him east to Manitoba, North Dakota, and Minnesota, and he read selections from his poetry. In the winter of 1913 he went to the Pacific coast. He went twice to the Icelandic celebrations in Wynyard, and the second time, in 1914, my mother accompanied him. She went east to Winnipeg and North Dakota in 1911. Then there was the memorable trip to Iceland in 1917, which rejuvenated him both physically and mentally. In 1926 his friends came and took him to Winnipeg for medical consultations. Dr. Pálsson came for him and my father and I travelled home together in August of that year.

Life did not seem to be so rushed in the olden days as it is now. While there were the cattle and the hay to work at, there was not as much steady work during the summer. In the first war years, everyone began ploughing their land and planting grain, thus changing the nature of farmwork. Our home was on my grandmother's homestead property. My father took land northeast of it, which was all hayland. Later, when he got a little money, he bought land beside the river and south of the home. And all that did was add to their cares and difficulties late in life. People were starting to clear land for growing crops then. As the years passed, my father's health began to fail. My mother remained a healthy person. It was in early December 1926, and we were both at home, when my father felt faint. I barely reached him in time to keep him from falling. The doctor said he had suffered a stroke but it was so mild that he did not lose consciousness. Many things were on his mind that he felt he had to finish. He had promised to compose the poetry for a cantata, and he still had some work left on Þiðrandi and more things. His right hand was weak, so I tried to write for him and he finished that which he was most anxious to do. By spring he was able to walk a bit, with help at first, and later could manage to get around with a cane, but he was an altogether different man, both in mind and body. On Sunday, August 9, 1927,

Thorstína Jackson showed some Icelandic pictures in the old house and several older people from the district attended. The next day an unexpected telegram arrived with the news that one of my father's best friends, Jakob Norman, was coming to visit from Wynyard, Saskatchewan. They spent only a short time together that evening, for while my mother and I were doing the outside chores, we were called in and told that my father had suffered a stroke. The doctor was called, but it was to no avail, as he died a few hours later, in the arms of his friend, so to speak. He had been granted his wish, as he wrote in his poem "Við Verkalok" ["At Close of Day"]:

> And offer the world at last my reconciling hand
> —when the sun sets.

When Jakob was asked why he had chosen to come at that time and had arrived on that very day, he replied he had dreamt a dream, which he interpreted as meaning that he should hurry if he wished to see his friend alive.

A long time before that, my father had ordered a casket from an Icelander who was a carpenter in the district. He wanted a casket similar to the one that had been made for my brother Gestur. The grave was lined with concrete and put in order as well as possible, and so he was laid to rest in the yard [cemetery], as mentioned in one poem: "and it is a short way over to the yard." It is on the family plot on the other side of the river on his sister's land, right on the bank of the Secret River, as he would have chosen. My mother stayed on in her home with our brother Jakob. She died in 1940 at the ripe old age of eighty-one. She came to visit me, took sick, and died from her illness just a few days later. She had been exceedingly healthy and devoted her strength until her last days to providing for her family and home. A year before she died, she had the misfortune to fall and break her hip. I have always felt this verse was so appropriate for her:

> All life will be open, while mind and hand
> and heart are able to work,
> and the grave is sweet for a fearless soul
> and it is good to return to one's own.

We humbly bless your memory, our parents, and give thanks for all your care and company on life's way. To you, my father, for the inheritance of noble ideals you have left to us. And to you, my mother, for the warmth you gave to our home, and your energy, which enabled our father to achieve great works.

—*Translated by Nina Campbell*

GUNNAR BJÖRNSSON &
INGIBJÖRG ÁGÚSTÍNA JÓNSDÓTTIR

❖

BY VALDIMAR BJÖRNSSON,
EDITOR, MINNEAPOLIS, MINNESOTA

*"When my mother's love for her
Icelandic heritage is mentioned,
then truly my father is next in line."*

*A*s an editor for a weekly newspaper, it was often my task to write obituaries. Fortunately, I have never had to write about close relatives until now—my mother is deceased but my father is still alive.

My mother was seventy-one when she died on August 19, 1949. My father will be eighty-three this year and he was born on August 17, 1872.

My mother's name was Ingibjörg Ágústína, the daughter of Jón Jónsson, a farmer at Hóll in Hörðudalur, Dalasýsla, and his wife Halldóra Baldvinsdóttir. Jón Sveinbjörnsson was my great-grandfather and his family came from Skagafjörður, while my grandmother Halldóra's family was from Miðdalir in Dalasýsla. The twin brothers, my grandfather Jón and Teitur, managed the farm at Hóll after their father died. In 1883 Jón moved to

America with a large group of people. At the time, my mother was not quite five years old.

The family came to Winnipeg and my grandfather built a log house during the first summer on the banks of the Red River where the Canadian National Railway Station now stands. He worked, as so many other immigrants did in those years, for the railway company. There were eleven Jón Jónssons on the work crew and they were known to the foreman only by a number. It was then that my grandfather chose Hördal as his last name, derived from Hörðudalur, and later it became Hurdal in English. The family, Jón and Halldóra, and their children—Jón, Helga, Ingibjörg Ágústína (my mother), Hjörtur and Sigríður (twins), Þorgerður, and Ása—were all born in Winnipeg. During the first summer they lived mostly on fish caught in the Red River.

My grandfather thought he would provide better for a large family as a farmer and soon moved to the Þingvalla colony in Saskatchewan, close to the town of Churchbridge, 560 kilometres northwest of Winnipeg. In 1890 my grandfather became a widower. My mother was only twelve years old when she lost her mother. From that day forward, my mother worked for her keep. She did not go to school for long. She worked in homes in the district and in Winnipeg. My grandfather moved back to Winnipeg with his seven children shortly after my grandmother died.

Mother received some education in Winnipeg. She was confirmed at the Lutheran church by Rev. Jón Bjarnason in 1892, but, for the most part, studied the catechism with Björn B. Jónsson, who was a student in theology. Rev. Björn B. Jónsson, a minister in Minnesota at the time, married my parents a few years later. He was a minister in Minnesota at the time, and the nephew of Kristján Fjallaskáld (the mountain poet).[1]

---

[1] Kristján Jónsson (1842–1869) was a leading poet in nineteenth-century Iceland. (Ed.)

My mother was twenty-three years old when she left Winnipeg in 1901. She went first to Minneapolis and stayed there for a summer with a female friend who had moved there from Winnipeg with her husband, Hjörtur Lárusson, a musician. Then Mother moved to the village of Minneota, which was 250 kilometres southwest of Minneapolis, because she had an offer to work in what was known as the "Large Store." It was operated by Ólafur Arngrímsson (Anderson) from Búastaðir in Vopnafjörður. She worked at that store until she married my father, Gunnar Björnsson, on March 20, 1903.

Mother took on a family, so to speak, from the day of her wedding. There was Kristín Benjamínsdóttir, my grandmother, who always lived with her son. There was also an old man, Þorbergur Guðbrandsson, who was a sort of a protégé of my father. Soon, another young man was added to the family. He was Sveinn Oddson, a printer and a new arrival from Reykjavík. Father hired him to work on the publication of the monthly Icelandic periodical *Vínland*, which was printed in my father's printing office. A newlywed modern woman of today would have found this task too much to take on, but my mother's calm demeanour was ever present.

Every single person believes that his mother's good qualities are invaluable and indescribable and that is certainly ingrained in everyone's nature. Never have I heard weaker praise about any man than when it is said that he loves his mother. It is difficult to describe, with impartiality, one's own mother. I have always thought that my mother's calm demeanour was among the strongest forces in her life, along with poise, patience, and unassuming modesty. She was skilful, industrious, and extremely capable. She was also cheerful and a wonderful conversationalist.

The same can truly be said about my parents and their six children who survived in the same way as what President Eisenhower said about his family when he was reminiscing about his youth: "Of course we were poor, but we didn't know it then." There was never enough of anything and I always admire my mother when I compare the conditions she had to deal with to what is now common. There was no running water in the house. We fetched drinking water in a pail from the well of Snorri Högnason, a neighbour who lived close by. Rainwater from the roof, which was pumped out of a cistern under the kitchen floor, was used for laundry and bathwater.

The three children born first were boys and their clothes were passed down, from Hjálmar to Valdimar to Björn. Each grew into the other's clothes, as was common in many places, and my mother sewed all the clothes. Then a girl was born, who was named Halldóra after her maternal grandmother. She died after a few months from pneumonia, which doesn't kill anyone in this age of wonder drugs. Next, two girls were born, Helga and Stefanía, and the last child, Jón, was born in 1919 when my mother was just over forty.

Mother cared for her large family with continuous energy, affection, and exceptional patience, true motherly love, and sacrifice. Grandmother died in 1920, nearly eighteen years after my parents married. Five years later, my parents moved to St. Paul, the capital city of Minnesota, when my father was appointed to the State Tax Commission. The three younger children moved with them but we, the three older brothers, stayed in Minneota. We continued at the print shop and published the paper in turn, as at least one or two of us were always there, while the third one attended the state university in Minneapolis. Thus all three of us finished our education, even though we did not go straight from preparatory school to university.

In the cities of St. Paul and Minneapolis, Mother experienced a better standard of living that lasted throughout the rest of her life. She missed her friends from her earlier years in Minneota and always returned there during the first summers after they moved to the big city. She was an outgoing person and she kept up her loyalty to the church and her religious beliefs in the Twin Cities as she had done in her hometown. She was a Christian woman by nature. Grandmother taught us the following grace: "Heavenly Father, bless us and these your gifts which we accept from your loving kindness, for Jesus Christ our Lord, Amen," whereas Mother let us read the grace. She urged us to attend church, no less after we were adults than when we were children.

The only Icelandic society in Minneapolis and St. Paul was the women's club, Hekla. Mother, of course, took on duties of the executive and, by doing that, she satisfied her desire to celebrate her heritage. Mother truly cherished her Icelandic descent. Her work in the English-speaking society of the International Institute in St. Paul showed this clearly. The Minnesota Icelanders' participation in the display and work in the Festival of Nations, the celebration of different ethnic groups, just over thirty in all, was due in large part to my mother's hard work.

She was always needlessly upset about her lack of formal education. She often felt inferior on that level, but it was unfounded. Others could not have done better than she on the few occasions that she dared to speak publicly—which was usually Father's place—as she told "foreigners" about Iceland and the Icelandic heritage. During the latter years of her life, her love for the Icelandic heritage, which was always considerable, grew stronger. It was a pleasure for her to reminisce about her two trips to Iceland. My parents went home to the

Alþingi [the Icelandic Parliament] celebration in 1930 and later, in 1940, the Icelandic National League and the Icelandic Government invited them to Iceland.

When my mother's love for her Icelandic heritage is mentioned, then truly my father is next in line. He was an Icelander through and through from the day he was born in Másskel, a small farm next to Sleðabrjót in Jökulsárshlíð in Norður Múlasýsla, August 17, 1872. His mother, a domestic servant, Kristín Benjamínsdóttir, descended from a family from Þingeyjarsýsla. His father, Björn Björnsson from Hallbjarnastaðir in Skriðdalur, Ásmundsson Hallgrímsson from Sandfell,[2] was at that time a labourer at Hvanná in Jökuldalur.

Father barely remembers Iceland from his youth, as he was not quite four years old when he moved with his mother during the summer of 1876. I will probably never know a man who was more Icelandic than he was. Since my parents were brought up in America, I find it odd how they and many others became so truly Icelandic. Father has always spoken the language as if he never left Iceland—the accent, the choice of words, concepts, sentence structures, spirit: all Icelandic. He held onto it despite the fact that he worked as an editor of an English newspaper. Never has his knowledge of Icelandic been a hindrance to him, but, rather, the opposite. In my opinion, it has increased his understanding of English. His editorials in that language were considered the most outstanding among the weekly newspapers in Minnesota for many years.

A large part of my father's heritage came from the poetry my grandmother taught him. The intellectual heritage was what we inherited from our grandmother. Its monetary value could never be estimated but it was a priceless treasure.

---

[2] The grandfather Björn was Ásmundur's son, and Ásmundur was the son of Hallgrímur from Sandfell. (Ed.)

When thinking about Father, I find Grandmother's courage and self-sacrifice moving. She arrived penniless with this little boy as her only possession. She worked to support him, living first in a turf house and working for a while for a Norwegian farmer north of Minneota. It was there that Father learned to speak the Norwegian Valdres dialect, which he never forgot. Father began early on to help his mother and relieve some of her burden. He worked with her as a sheepherder and was an errand boy among the Icelandic farmers in the district west of town. He first went to school in the east district, upstairs in the house of Björn at Stórhóll—Björn Gíslason Danneborgsmaður, from Haugastaðir in Vopnafjörður. He attended elementary school in Marshall, twenty kilometres east of Minneota. For one winter, Grandmother moved there with him, rented a room on the second floor over a store, and worked for their keep. At this time, he was close to confirmation age. He also went to school in Minneota and almost finished secondary school.

Minneota had a population of a few hundred people and nearly every home had a milking cow at the time. Father had a job as a cow herder during the summers at a pasture just north of town. He worked as a carpenter for a few years for Loftur Jónsson from Lundarbrekka in Bárðardalur and for Kristján Schram from Reykjavík. He then worked in a store, went to a business college in Quincy, Illinois, for a winter, and studied law for two years with Kristján Magnússon Gíslason from Búðardalur, a lawyer in Minneota. In 1895 he began his career as a journalist when he became co-editor of the *Minneota Mascot*, the weekly newspaper, which was established in 1891. He quit that position after two years but bought the paper in 1901 and owned it for more than forty years. It was there that he made his sons into printers and editors.

My father was a loving father from the start. That can probably be said about most fathers but it was actually a noteworthy characteristic of his. He always remembered his children at home when he was away on a trip. His trips were many since he became involved early on in politics. Even if he was away for only a few days he would send his children postcards and letters. He was a generous man, always wanting to give more than he had. It was in his nature to share with others.

My father was a representative in the state legislature in St. Paul for two consecutive years, sitting from 1913 to 1915 for Lyon county, the southwest district in the state. He was the leader of the Republican Party in the state in 1914, in addition to being one of the main supporters of the party in his home county. He was appointed to the State Tax Commission in 1925 and held that position for ten years, and was appointed to the State Board of Tax Appeals when that commission was established in 1939 and reinstated by the government in 1945 and 1951. He retired in his eighty-third year on April 1, 1955, after nearly thirty years of service.

I shall not go on about my father's abilities as a leader in his home county or outside. Those leadership skills come naturally to an editor, especially in a small town where he sat on the school board and was the president of the editorial association in the state. He was the president of the Icelandic Lutheran congregation in Minneota for many years, served often at the Synods assembly, travelled around the Icelandic districts in Canada and the United States, giving speeches, and spoke at Icelandic celebrations and at other such gatherings. My father has usually been eloquent, both in his spoken language and in his numerous articles, which he wrote as an editor for many decades. His mother was witty and her comments always hit their mark, and my father was exposed to this characteristic of his mother's from an early age. He used this talent brilliantly both in conversation and in public speaking—humour that was both witty but refined. He always had a comeback and was an influential speaker, weaving together effortlessly his natural wit and seriousness.

He was a handsome man with a deep voice. He could playfully shift from jest to sarcasm, from even-tempered speech to thundering accusations. He was an outstanding public speaker, both in Icelandic and English. Although he hasn't composed much poetry, the inclination toward it is deeply rooted in his makeup. He loves poetry and knows a great number of poems, verses, literary pearls, and even ballads. He is equally knowledgeable in English and Icelandic literature. His poetic sense always left a mark on his speech and in his writing.

My father always seemed to be able to buy books regardless of financial circumstances. He has good taste in literature, as can be seen in his selections of English, Icelandic, and Norwegian books. He often read the Icelandic sagas and many other things aloud for us children. If anyone was bored with the reading, he was a master at telling us his own stories. He has been mostly a self-educated man, but so widely read that he has always been an equal to those who have a degree or a title.

My parents made certain that all their six children had a university education, and they deserve our gratitude for that. Their belief in the profound value of the accomplishment of the spirit was an invaluable gift to their children. This is the true inheritance that Icelanders passed on to their descendants who trace their roots to the nation, which Matthías Jochumsson (1835 to 1920) once described as "a nation of history, of poets and heroes."

This precious inheritance my parents have given to their six children, which includes all the best characteristics of Icelandic immigrants to America: eagerness to learn, an inextinguishable longing for education, love of literature and poetry, respect for justice, and the will to sacrifice something for it. At the core of this was the respect ingrained in us for the Icelandic language and its key role in the preservation of Icelandic culture.

—*Translated by Árný Hjaltadóttir*

GUTTORMUR ÞORSTEINSSON & BIRGITTA JÓSEPSDÓTTIR

❖

BY REV. GUTTORMUR GUTTORMSSON, MINNEOTA, MINNESOTA

"I have deep respect for the baðstofa culture, which characterized life in Iceland when I was a child."

*K*rossavík is beautiful, and the hayfield there is extremely large," says antiquarian Sigurður Vigfússon in an account of his travels in eastern Iceland during the summer of 1890.[1] He speaks here of my childhood home, Krossavík in Vopnafjörður.

Krossavík is mentioned in the history of Iceland at different times over the centuries. Geitir Lýtingsson and his kinsmen lived there during the Saga Age,[2] and 150 years ago the farm was the residence of county magistrate Guðmundur Pétursson ("the Rich").[3] He is mentioned in various sources from the time and, although these accounts of him differ in records that have been passed down, it is my belief that he was a noteworthy official who loved his nation. It should be noted that Guðmundur

---

[1] *The Icelandic Archeological Society Yearbook*, 1893.
[2] The story of the feud between the inhabitants of Krossavík and Hof is in *Vopnfirðinga Saga*. (Trans.)
[3] Guðmundur Pétursson lived from 1748 to 1811. (Trans.)

was on a voyage doing business for his homeland when he died as the result of a fall in Leith, Scotland, in 1811.

There is no doubt about the beauty of Krossavík. The midnight sun still casts a dreamlike, radiant glory over the sea, fields, and mountains in my mind's eye when I think back to my boyhood years spent in this place. But the land was no longer the seat of chieftains when Sigurður came to visit it. It was divided into thirds and three turf farmhouses stood in this large field of which he speaks.

In the farthest inland of the three lived my parents, Guttormur Þorsteinsson ("the Strong"), who was Guðmundur's grandson, and his wife Birgitta Jósepsdóttir from Syðravík. When Sigurður came to Krossavík, we children were allowed to be present in the sitting room and to listen to the conversation. My father showed him the tableware from his grandfather's household, a silver knife and fork, along with the greatest treasure of all: a gold spoon. "I would have wished to have been the maker of this," said Sigurður when he saw the spoon. He was a goldsmith. My parents did not own any other heirloom from the "Krossavík riches." Sigurður bought the tableware for the museum in Reykjavík.[4]

My father was born in Krossavík around 1838. As a young man, he travelled to Copenhagen, most likely around 1860, and stayed there for two years, where he became a watchmaker and took lessons in swimming, German, song, and playing an instrument. The instrument, a guitar, had vanished from the scene before my time. But my father must have used his time in Copenhagen well, for he repaired watches and clocks for the rest of his life, though he was paid little for his work. He taught us boys to swim as he had learned but this method is no longer used. The eldest siblings learned Danish from him and

---

[4] The National Museum, *Þjóðminjasafnið*. (Trans.)

he also taught us to sing hymns. For a time he was lead singer at *Hofkirkja* [Hof Church], though not for long. Krossavík is a long way from the church and travel is difficult as there are a number of rivers to cross to get there. My mother was born in the village of Siglufjörður. I do not know the year. Her father was Jósep Jónsson, who was from Syðravík, the next farm inland from Krossavík. He was young when he began working in the stores and then sailed to Copenhagen. Later, he was a store manager at Örum and Wulf's shop in Siglufjörður, as I recall, and then moved back to Sydravík, where he died. At around the age of confirmation, my mother went to Vopnafjörður. She enjoyed telling stories of her time there, where she learned handwork and also studied in the household of Rev. Halldór, provost at Hof Church at that time. She had, of course, learned Danish previously. She was very well educated according to the standards of the time, knowing, among other things, how to play chess, something she later taught to us. She won an award for a piece of her weaving, which was displayed, I remember, in Reykjavík. I heard about it as a child.

My mother was not a tall woman. She was slender and delicately built, energetic, blue-eyed with auburn hair, and was considered to be beautiful. She was always courteous in her everyday conduct, but gave her opinion clearly and without hesitation when it came down to it.

My father was of slightly less than average height, but well-built, quite strong and a hard worker, as I remember him, and, above all, he was never idle. He was dark-haired and his hair thinned early on, as was typical in that family. He was a quiet man, introverted by nature and somewhat reserved.

An acquaintance of mine, Ágúst Vopni, brother of Jón Vopni from Winnipeg, lived for a time with his mother on the lower farm in Krossavík. He sent me, this winter, the following description of my parents:

> The first thing that men became aware of when they met Guttormur was respect for his temperate manner of action and courtesy. He was customarily a man of few words and let small matters pass him by. He was a good singer; he took delight in song and was often invited to wedding celebrations to keep up the festive spirit, which came very naturally to him, after he had tasted a little wine; it was then that his witty humour really came out. Guttormur's farm was well built. All was kept neat and tidy by the gentle and well-mannered mistress of the house, Birgitta Jósepsdóttir. She was a good woman and God-fearing. Guttormur Þorsteinsson and Birgitta Jósepsdóttir's household was a model of good conduct, cleanliness and hospitality.

Here the sense of the friendship may be easily seen. The description is not far from the truth. And it is true that my father had a glass on occasions where alcohol was served, just as was common practice in those days, but he was never a drunkard.

Baðstofa Culture

My parents were married around 1890. Their household, the farthest inland of the three farms at Krossavík, was a typical turf farmhouse, with timber panelling on the front.

The *stofa* [sitting room] was located at the front of the house and the *baðstofa* [living quarters] was in the innermost part of the farmhouse. It was bitterly cold in the winter, especially when the storms hit, and, therefore, the cows were kept beneath the living quarters for heating purposes. Such an arrangement was looked down upon, even in the country, but if it meant life or death, then there was no other choice. Furnace heating was unheard of. The cold set in for the longest out in the *gestastofa* [guest room], but it had its own attraction despite this. It was there that the cultural heritage was kept. Pictures of splendid houses in Copenhagen decorated the panelling. Cupboards were full of books and papers, both Icelandic and Danish. There was reading material both old and new, scholarly works, songbooks, old sagas, poems, and periodicals, in both languages. But there were no Danish novels as far as I can remember, and certainly no *rímur*-poetry [Icelandic ballads].

Readings took place in the baðstofa on winter nights, though not continuously. The weaving stool took priority over all reading, if weaving went on into the night. Sometimes the eldest boys were studying and then they were the readers. Or perhaps they would read something in Danish for our father as an exercise; but this was not actually baðstofa reading. I heard *Njáls Saga* read twice in the baðstofa. Other reading material included stories from books both old and new, scholarly writings, news, or newspaper articles. Newspapers from America were sometimes borrowed and read with eagerness. Here was something altogether new, something full of great achievements, and it filled the mind with wonder.

But rímur-poems were something we never heard. There was an old man named Jósías living with us and he knew a great number of these rímur-poems and other pieces of folk-poetry. He would often hum to himself one or another of these while he was in the baðstofa. Jósías owned one single book from which he was sometimes asked to read for those around him and that really pleased him. The book was Sveinbjörn's translation of the epic *The Odyssey*. He read the book through at least twice for us.

Sometimes teachers who travelled the countryside would stay with us during the winter, for as long as a month at a time, and they gave the eldest children the basic principles in education. This undoubtedly fuelled their interest in studying. But my siblings must have received most of their education themselves from the books, just as other youngsters did out in the country in those days.

Another form of education in the baðstofa was daily conversation. People did not sit silently at their wool-working when there was a pause in the reading. And, of course, the neighbours were talked of—who can avoid it? The world of men would become a dull place indeed if this topic of discussion is ever discontinued. But for the baðstofa chatter to have been idle gossip or slander was out of the question. Conversations were many-faceted. Almost anything between heaven and earth could be discussed, including things one had read in books or experienced personally. We never tired of hearing our father tell us of his stay in Copenhagen and the splendours of that great city. It was just the same with reading. That which one of us had read became, as often as not, the property of the entire household. Learning came to life because it became the topic of discussion. Essays in *Fjölnir* and various other materials, which I neither read nor heard in my youth, were nonetheless well-known subjects to me when I read them later. Their content had come to me through the discussions at home in the baðstofa.

It could be said that daily conversation is more or less educational the world over. I acknowledge this. But the content depends on circumstances. In sparsely populated rural Iceland, baðstofa conversations had a special meaning and a special value. There were no cinemas, no concert halls, and schools were rare or non-existent. The household had to teach and entertain itself. The people on Icelandic farms did this unstintingly, both the members of the household and also any visitors who happened to drop by.

Poetry was also recited, both old and new. The most popular poets among us and, of course, many others in eastern Iceland were Kristján Jónsson and Páll Ólafsson. Many of their works were on every man's lips, excerpts and whole poems, and there were always new verses to be heard from the people. My father put great value on poetry and had good taste too, I think. He needed to sample each poem like a new dish, taste it, see how it rolled around the mouth, and told us unhesitatingly of its flaws if the verse was not good. I think he would have been a good teacher, in literature in particular. He was especially patient when answering our questions, which were naturally often childlike at that time.

Piety was cultivated through the same means as then was typical across the land. My father read *Pétur's Sermons* on Sunday. Meditations were read at night during the work week in the winter and there were always accompanying hymns. The *Passion Hymns* were read during Lent and I saw tear-stained eyes now and again when these hymns were sung.

I doubt that any religious work, other than the Bible, has ever found deeper roots in the hearts of the common people than the *Passion Hymns*. Fine and easily understandable religious works exist in English, such as *Pilgrim's Progress* by Bunyan, or *Serious Call* by Law, or *Imitation of Christ* by Thomas à Kempis, in English translation, and other books of the same type. They are highly praised in writing; but I will solemnly swear that I have never heard a single person quote a word out of them except for two women who told me of Bunyan's *Pilgrim's Progress;* they had read the book *in Icelandic.*

But Hallgrímur's *Passion Hymns* were on every man's lips. It was quite common for men to quote these hymns, recite passages out of them, or aphorisms—even whole verses—to support their arguments, whatever the topic of conversation might be.

Our mother went to great lengths to teach us religion and good behaviour, speaking often from her own heart about her beliefs. She could be tender or strict, depending on what was required. Decency was a heartfelt matter for her. Anything but good behaviour was sharply reprimanded and if we children were rude, then a slap on the face was certain. The slap was delivered by whichever of us siblings stood closest by. That was a rule in our home. I remember well how my mother urged us to behave properly, and she did so with cheerfulness and kindness. We needed that.

New Currents

During these years, the nation was in a time of progressive thinking. Some changes may not have been a step forward, but most were necessary and good. I often heard men speak of various strange ideas and customs of the "old folks," as they called the generations before. Superstition was in decline. Belief in *afturgöngur* [the walking dead] had, as far as I know, vanished, or all but so. The *huldufólk* [hidden people] had become, for the most part, a thing of story. But *svipir* [apparitions], *vofur* [ghosts], and *fylgjur* [following-spirits] still had a firm hold in the national psyche. "No such thing as ghosts," my father used to say sometimes, but he was the only one I ever heard make such a strong statement.

Various new publications to come out were clearly headed in the direction of progress. The new hymn book was a rich addition to the field of Icelandic religious literature and became popular at once, although the *Passion Hymns* still held their own place of honour. At about the same time, several pamphlets came out on scientific matters. They were called *Sjálfsfræðarinn [The Self-Educator]*, as I recall. These were not read aloud, but the material in them was discussed in the baðstofa so that all might benefit.

The volumes of Jónas Helgason's song collection had, I believe, all come out by then, and its influence was spreading. Gunnlaugur Oddsen, son of Vilhjálmur the saddler, was then the organist in Hof Church, or had been. He lived at this time with his father at Hellisfjörubakkar, a cottage near Krossavík, down by the sea. Gunnlaugur was hired to teach singing to the young men in Krossavík and in this group were my older siblings and other youths. Lessons took place weekly, for two winters, in our sitting room. We younger children were permitted to be present. Gunnlaugur taught us songs out of Jónas's collection, in three and four voices; he had a flute to "take the note" and "mark time," but no other instrument was used.

We became so taken with these songs that we forgot the cold. The songs we learned were then sung in the winter evenings, in all voices, throughout the week. My eldest brothers conducted these songs and all the children joined in. The songs became the property of the household. We then began to learn the voices for the hymns as well. It was as if we had taken the hand of heaven.

The Reykjavík edition of the Sagas of Icelanders was, at this time, being released and it was inexpensive and popular. In all likelihood, it increased the readership of this literature considerably. One may say that these books helped to put the final

nails in the coffin of rímur-poetry. There is no doubt that rímur-
poetry had its own value in its own time. We would sometimes
come close to missing rímur-poetry at times, when we heard
somewhere a captivating battle poem such as the following verse:

Féll á skaftið fleinaraftur fast af megni;
á bak aftur því datt þegni,
þrotinn kraftur hjörs í regni.

Spear was shattered, shaft undone
with mighty force;
Warrior fell, was downed perforce,
sword disabled, cruel fate would run its course.[5]

But then the ancient sagas arrived, with explanations of the
meanings of the verses in the back of the book. The old poets
became understandable! Some of this verse we read here, some
in America. Here was the origin, the hero's soul in all its original
strength, just as here in Egil's "Head-Ransom":[6]

Beit fleinn floginn,
þá var friðr loginn,
vas almr dreginn,
varð ulfr feginn.

Soaring shaft bit,
the peace was split,
bows were drawn,
the wolf looked on.[7]

But after this, rímur-poetry fell out of favour. These ballads
weren't what they used to be; they lost their thunder, so to
speak. But there were still limits to the enthusiasm that these
ancient poet-heroes awoke. They seem to have been so frightfully

[5] Trans. David Gíslason. Unless indicated otherwise, all verses are translated by David Gislason.
[6] A piece Egill Skallagrímsson composed for King Eirík in order to save his own head. (Trans.)
[7] Stanza 13, lines 1–4. In modern editions of *Egil's Saga*, the last two lines are often inverted. (Trans.)

attached to their wolf and birds of carrion, for to sate the wolf, gorge the raven, but chop up the menfolk—this was the main topic of every heroic lay! There was another shortcoming that was little better: when these powerful poems were translated into modern language as prose, they lost all their strength. They became watered down and there was no longer any incitement to battle left in them.

Many people of today are worried about the violent content of the coloured picture comics here in America. They think that in these comics may be hidden one of the main causes for the epidemic of immorality and ill-will that has spread out in this land among our young people. Now, it may be that there is something to this. But I believe that rímur-poetry and the old sagas are rather similar to these coloured pictures. Each has plenty of coarse material in them, such as negligence, brutality, robbery, plundering, and murder. Both befit the prophet's words: "Your hands are covered in blood." The examples are not a perfect analogy but the entire subject is worthy of consideration and investigation. But if it were true, then why has our literary heritage—the bloody old sagas and rímur-poetry that have entertained the young generation for centuries—not turned us into a nation of beasts?

To sum up, I have deep respect for the baðstofa culture that characterized life in Iceland when I was a child. It brought together knowledge and hard work, and it caught the educational currents, both old and new, in everyday life, enriching two generations at once. The home was a workplace, school, church, concert hall, and hospital, all under the same roof. The baðstofa brought harmony into the household.

No one should interpret my words to mean that I wish to do away with all the modern technology of today and squeeze humanity into a farm-hovel with a turf roof overhead and cows stabled beneath. Of course not, and even if I did, progress would still go its own way despite this. But I want to say that those who experienced the baðstofa culture adapted in reverse proportion the old parable: they invested very well this one little talent with which they were entrusted.[8] And let them now do better in proportion, those who have been given the two talents or five, or, in other words, those who had greater riches in their life.

Hard Times and Heartache

Rural life was no paradise. Survival has always been a difficult struggle in Iceland and not least of all in that quarter century in question here. One disaster came after another during this time: ash-fall,[9] snowy winter, cold spring, pack ice. The "frost winter" of 1880 and the "hard spring" of 1882 were events of which I often heard. Pack ice lay up on the shore twice within my memory, first in 1888 and later in 1891, if I remember correctly. I remember the latter spring well. A great amount of snow came along with the ice during the summer months. The sheep were driven west over the Hof River, out to where the heath lay under the sun, and were saved there. The cows were on half their usual hay rations. We boys would go down to the sea, to a spot on the coast where the sea was rather deep and seaweed covered the low, flat rocks. We cut the seaweed up and brought it, cold and dripping wet, back to the farm. This method of haymaking saved the cows and the milk they were able to give. Grown men went out onto the ice and killed a few seals there. Old and young joined hands together in the battle against hardship and hunger.

On top of all else, this was an era of progress. Development is not to be taken lightly. It creates pain and difficulty for men,

---

[8] In the original Icelandic: "Hann ávaxtaði mæta vel þetta eina, litla pund, sem honum var trúað fyrir. Geri þeir nú betur að tiltölu, sem þegið hafa pundin tvö eða fimm." (As noted by reader Pat Odegard.)
[9] The volcano Askja erupted in 1875. (Trans.)

losses as well as gains, and it even goes the wrong way at times. In addition, it moves forward in two directions: one spiritual, the other technical. These two must keep up with each other in some way if things are to go well. Here in the New World, technical development is far ahead of the spiritual, say knowledgeable men, something hardly looked on as a cause for celebration.

But in Iceland, the problem was just the opposite, as the mind was far ahead of technology. With growing knowledge and appreciation for art, people began to make greater demands of life. They yearned for greater comfort, a more wholesome environment, more schools for the children, and a better standard of living in all respects. But it was precisely during these years that the weather was as "morose and snappish" as Glámur of old.[10] Most tried to eke out a living and get ahead and there was no lack of trying. Many reforms were discussed and while some were never acted upon, others were tossed around for a year or two before tumbling down like Sisyphus's stone.[11] Ill-conceived ideas and ignorance often seem to have joined hands together. This effort was, above all, in its infancy.

Much was written and discussed on the subject, and the blame was often thrown on the man who had the most difficulties. He was accused of laziness, negligence, and wastefulness—a comfort that helped him about as much as a slap in the face. It was hardly a cure for the disappointment and the weariness.

The Icelandic nation had, of course, lived through worse years than these. It was still unbeaten, "unconquered," as it is called, though the battle might be hard. The captain of the ship that brought us west across the sea said he was unable to understand how well people seemed to be doing in Seyðisfjörður, "even as cold and barren as things looked there."[12] This was not

---

[10] A bad-tempered shepherd in *Grettir's Saga* whose ghost later plagues the farm of his former employer. (Trans.)

[11] According to Greek mythology, Sisyphus was a man condemned by the gods to spend all eternity rolling a boulder up a mountain again and again. (Trans.)

[12] "Dómar um Íslendinga [Judgement about Icelanders]," *Lögberg*, Sept. 16, 1893.

the only factor behind the apprehension Icelanders felt during this time. The causes were two and united as one; I have named them both: harsh times and growing demands for better living conditions.

It often happens that some zealous stirring up of mind or mindset grips thousands of men at the same time, even whole nations. Such was the case for the Icelandic nation, I believe, shortly before we went west. Most men yearned to get ahead, but got nowhere. That which was gained one year was lost in the next. "Whatever Providence reluctantly gives me, the Devil takes away again in great chunks," one of our fellow countrymen sometimes said here in the New World when he was drunk. I think he must have taken the expression with him from Iceland, for the same disappointment and resentment were something I noticed often in the talk of men in my district at the time, though the words they used were a little milder.

Even Matthías Jochumsson—and who has loved Iceland better than he?—seems to have been caught up for a moment or landed in this mindset, which was passing. He composed a scathing poem on the land of his ancestors, "A cross, like other timber, falls in time."[13] The poem flew around the whole countryside. One verse went as follows:

> Hrafnfundna land,
> munt þú ei hentugast hröfnum?
> Héðan er bent vorum stöfnum,
> hrafnfundna land![14]

---

[13] An Icelandic proverb meaning "even the most trustworthy-seeming may fail" or "no one is infallible." (Trans. D.G.)

[14] The poem "Volaða land [Wretched-land]" by Matthías Jochumsson (1835–1920) was first printed in *Lögberg* (now *Lögberg-Heimskringla*) on July 18, 1888. This is the last stanza of the poem, and captures its spirit. In the original text of *Foreldrar mínir,* two lines from the last stanza (the first and the fourth) are mixed with the third stanza (lines three and four): "Hrafnfundna land!/ Hrákasmíð hrynjandi skánar,/hordregið örverpi Ránar!/ Hrafnfundna land!" The following sentence in the original text reads as follows: "Víkur hér orðum að landskjálftunum," thus explaining how the two lines refer to earthquakes. (Ed.)

> Ravenfound land,
> are you not best suited ravens?
> My people must seek other havens,
> ravenfound land!

In another verse, "clawed by hoarfrost-giant nails" was written. This may refer to the streaks that are seen widely in the cliffs there back home, created by the weight of shifting gravel in the Ice Age. Of course, the poet later made amendments for the harsh words:

> Þeir segja ég hafi hrópað fár
> og heift yfir þínar slóðir;
> en brenni mín sál um eilíf ár,
> ef ann ég þér ekki, móðir!

> They say I've been known to curse and yell—
> with hatred my land to smother.
> But may I forever burn in Hell,
> if I love you not, my mother.

The poem is not quoted here to disparage him, nor the land, but rather to show the dismay that, at the time, could grip— though for no longer than the blink of an eye and only half-seriously—Matthías Jochumsson himself!

It must be mentioned, so that everything may be put in its proper prospective, that the discontent did not all come from one side. Old Iceland had its own fierce opponents as well, who spoke harshly about the New World agents, the emigrants, and the New World itself. The agents also let similar strong opinions fly about their own side of the story. "The accusations go both ways." "The difference is great," said one agent, when he met with men who were on the difficult journey over Hellisheiði in late winter: "In Iceland, we wade in the snow, but in America men wade in money." But *Þjóðólfur* fared no better in that it, too, exaggerated the truth.[15] These agents, said the paper, were seducing the people "west to the desert-plains of Canada, where everything burns and freezes." In my view, one is no worse than the other.

THE VOYAGE WEST

It was little wonder that Icelanders looked with great interest to the New World during those times. They received favourable reports from their fellow countrymen in the West. The letters from America travelled from farm to farm, and the Icelandic Winnipeg papers were widely read. These reports certainly had more effect on men's minds than the boasting of agents. The letter writers had clearly made a great effort, most of them, to tell of the new land, both its advantages and disadvantages. But the advantages always came out on top. That which tipped the scales was the hope and the joy that shone out from these letters. And the same was true of their newspapers. Western Icelanders never doubted for a moment that the new land had a magnificent future, whatever difficulties might arise in the short term. This unshakable trust in land and nation was well expressed in Einar Hjörleifsson's "Memory of New Iceland":[16]

> Þú ert land hins þróttmikla og nýja,
> þú varst aldrei fegri' en nú í dag.

> You are a country new and strong,
> and never lovelier than today.

It stood out from the weariness and hopelessness of Iceland.

---

[15] *Þjóðólfur*, the oldest newspaper to be printed in Iceland, was established in 1848. (Trans.)

[16] Einar Hjörleifsson Kvaran was an Icelandic writer and poet who spent ten years in Winnipeg as a newspaper editor. (Trans.)

There is no need to waste words; the desire to go to America gripped my mother and my father at last, just as it had so many others. Finances were difficult as there were ten children and our section of land was not enough to both support the family and pay labourers at the same time. At the very end, there was only one workwoman with us, and no man. The eldest boys were also then approaching twenty. I cannot recall that the mindset I described before particularly hindered the decision to leave. Everyone worked with zeal, since the work was always waiting for us. My father was working constantly, it seemed to me, as was my mother. It was not in their nature to turn a profit and definitely not at this time as it was difficult to avoid debts.

In the spring of 1893, the land was sold and preparations were made for the trip west with the children. My next-eldest brother, Þorsteinn, stayed behind at home. He had learned to play on the harmonium one winter in Seyðisfjörður and was now the organist at Hof Church, but a few years later he went west as well.

We had to wait for passage into midsummer. In the end, a coal freighter arrived from England, gathered emigrants from harbours in the north of the country, and brought the group to Seyðisfjörður. The line ship *Lake Huron* then took them straight from Seyðisfjörður to Québec. I have always regretted that we weren't allowed to stop in England.

We put out to sea on the second of August. The group travelling west on this occasion was large—525 in all. The ship followed the coast going west, and the last we saw of Iceland must have been Dyrhólaey. It seemed to me that men fell silent when they saw the land of their ancestors sink into the sea. "It is ill for them, who are bereft of a homeland," said Hrútur Herjólfsson.[17] He probably meant by this that such a man

---

[17] From *Njal's Saga*. The Icelander Hrútur Herjólfsson, then living in Norway, gives this as his explanation for wishing to return to his native land. (Trans.)

longed to be away when he was home, but home when he was out of the country. This was likely true for many an Icelander through the ages—and not least of all this group on the ship. All hope of earning a profit in Iceland had been lost for many people, and their belief in the future of the country likely along with it. But, as it says in the hymn:

> trú og von þótt vari skammt,
> þá varir ástin samt.

> though faith and hope be insecure,
> 'tis love that will endure.[18]

So it was in the hearts of those I knew best and, of course, many others. They still wished to be able to stand old *Frón*[19] in good stead in some way. On this ship I heard for the first time that phrase I have often heard since: "to not disgrace Icelanders."

My countrymen took care of this very well on the ship *Lake Huron*. The ship's captain bestowed much praise on this group when we arrived in the West. He said he had brought many groups of people across the Atlantic Ocean, but never a group as handsome, clean, and healthy as these Icelanders. This praise may be read in an article in *Lögberg*.

Death took its toll on the group, though. A woman died at sea in childbirth, Margrét Jónsdóttir from Vopnafjörður. In other respects, the trip west went very well. We had calm and mild weather all the way. The ship was not fast-moving and I recall that we were nine days at sea.

When the passengers were counted and the fares turned in, the last of the men came out of the bowels of the ship. He was an Icelander by the name of Hermann, later

---

[18] Excerpt from "Hymn 353" by Valdimar Briem (1848–1930), in *Sálmabók [Icelandic Hymnal]* (Reykjavík: Sigfús Eymundsson, 1886).
[19] A poetic term for Iceland. (Trans.)

called "Götuskellir," and I believe he got the nickname in America. Hermann had come aboard in the flood of people in Seyðisfjörður, and now there was no other choice but to bring him west. The guides for this group, Sigurður Christopherson and Sveinn Brynjólfsson, must have lent him the fare. Sigurður had with him on the ship an Icelandic horse and several sheep. Other Icelandic horses must also have come west later on.

The view was beautiful down the St. Lawrence River. The land spread out before us like a striped bedspread with the fields either harvest gold or a beautiful fresh green. However, I shall now speed up the trip. We came to Winnipeg on August 15. Many Icelanders came down to the "immigrant house" to welcome their fellow countrymen and ask for news from Iceland. Among the welcomers was Wilhelm Paulson, later an MLA in Saskatchewan. He was then in the prime of his life. Paulson stepped up on the edge of something raised in the hall to address the people and brought us the wonderful news that dinners were prepared free of charge for anyone who couldn't pay—"for no one goes hungry in this land," he said.

CHOICE OF HOME

The voyage to the promised land was now over, but another problem still remained: where in this country should we now go? My parents had always more or less intended to settle in Minnesota because many people from Vopnafjörður lived there, but discouraging reports of bankruptcy and unemployment came north from the United States. My father would not, in fact, have had a great deal of money to put into a bank, but he didn't like the look of it. Less was said of the depression in Canada but such difficulties must have been there, too. The agents and others scarcely mentioned it, as they were Canadians. Sigurður wanted to send us to the town of Brandon. What he saw in this advice, I don't know.

A few New Icelanders came to the "immigrant house." New Iceland, on the southwestern shores of Lake Winnipeg, was the oldest Icelandic settlement in western Canada, established in 1875, at the time when grasshoppers had eaten up all the vegetation on the prairie to the south in those regions. The shoreline seemed to the exploration party to be ideal for impoverished pioneers in other respects, as well. There were waters filled with fish, an abundance of forest for building houses and firewood, and pastureland all through the forests. However, after several years, great disputes arose over this choice of settlement and many people abandoned it and moved to North Dakota, the Argyle settlement, or to other towns. They did not have much good to say about New Iceland, and not entirely without cause. The settlement got a bad name. It was often called "north and down"[20] to go to New Iceland.

However, the settlement had its own supporters in those who continued the struggle when others fled and it was from this group of settlers that a long-bearded man spoke to the new arrivals. "It may well be," says he, "that the settlement is not as bustling as Argyle or Dakota, but it has its own future at hand and will become in the end the most successful of the new colonies." The man's message was convincing. Many people spoke of going north and settling there.

Sigurður, the agent, spoke decidedly against this advice. He had, during the pioneer years, settled on land eight kilometres south of Gimli, called Húsavík—the farms were given Icelandic names up north there, as they still are today. But Sigurður was not happy with his lot in New Iceland. He was among the first

---

[20] An Icelandic expression also meaning "go to hell." (Trans.)

men to move to the Argyle settlement and left the Húsavík land unsold. "Really!" says Sigurður. "To intend to go up to New Iceland, up in the mud and the flies! Impossible to deal with these people!"

However, an Icelander is stubborn. Our family went up to New Iceland with several others and stayed in Selkirk for a few days before getting passage north to Gimli on the steamboat *Colville*. My parents bought a little log cabin on the lakeshore, and lived there for three years, as I recall. By then the money was nearly exhausted and the children had to support themselves working for others, all except the three youngest. My mother mentioned later how painful it had been to send the children away, but it had to be so. Still, their home was our home all the same. We went back to our parents on weekends and as often as we could, whenever it was possible.

When my father came to the New World, it was as if a heavy burden had been lifted from him. Now the hardship was ended and he was debt-free again. He was talkative, sure of himself, and more outgoing than before. But the change was not entirely on the outside. He had kept his religious beliefs at home and never spoken a word against the faith, but now he confessed frankly that doubts had plagued him for years. Now those doubts were gone and his faith had been rekindled. It was in this light he lived for the rest of his days. There was a great deal of turmoil over religion in New Iceland and disputes arose over these issues, but he ignored all this and kept the faith that lived within him.

NEW ICELAND—DRAWBACKS

In New Iceland, there was no fear of bankruptcy for there were no banks. The settlement bore an interesting name: it was a new Iceland, with the same language and the same customs to a great extent. But the struggle for existence was less diffi-cult than at home, if men were satisfied with little—which was quite common. Forest and lake took care of immediate needs. To add to their income, men mainly sold fish, and sometimes cattle or meat, but many left home for part of the year to work at the fishing stations or they went "out to work" in towns, on the railroad, or with harvesting crews and so on. People were full of hope that some day they would enjoy prosperity.

There were disadvantages, too. The settlement was rather isolated. Settlers did not get a railroad up north before the turn of the century. Poplar forest lined the shore and it had its own uses, but the poplar has sometimes been called the "weed of the forest." The trees are easily cut down, but also fast-growing. When men clear such a forest, it is then also necessary to grub or to clear away roots just as diligently, otherwise roots will produce new shoots all around the stump and everything becomes a dense forest again after several years. But grubbing is time-consuming work—cleaning away the underbrush and tearing up roots and stumps.

In most places, though, the settlers had cleared away a fairly big area around their home. This clearing was called a *blettur* [21] and was cultivated like a hayfield in Iceland. Most often there would be a pause in this grubbing when the blettur had become several acres in size.

In many places, the forest impeded water drainage and standing water covered large areas in the spring and during rainstorms, making the roads nearly impassable and turning the uncultivated lands into swamps. In spite of this, road improve-ments progressed slowly. The mail came once a week, and less often during spring thaws.

---

[21] A blettur was a fenced-in, well-tilled piece of land, not far from the house. It may have been seeded to alfalfa and cut twice a year for hay. It could be reached from the road. (Trans.)

There is one dilemma still uncounted and by no means the smallest. Scientists have hypothesized that the ultimate battle here on earth will not be held between kingdoms or nationalities, but, rather, between life forms—man contends thus with the insects. And the insects will rise up to the fight. They keep themselves on track in that the generations are simply born, nourish themselves, breed, and die. It is man who has all kinds of digressions. I know nothing of the truth of this prophecy, but I could imagine that the instigator of this theory had fled from New Iceland during its pioneer days. The insects there were all-encroaching and lived a happy life. Those known as bedbugs live in dead wood; they are thus dangerous in log cabins and often make their rounds regardless of how well walls are cleaned and whitewashed—or so it was in those days.

But still worse were the flying insects. Mosquitoes (*múskítur*) arrived early in the summer in the billions and attacked men and beasts daily from evening to morning all the way into the autumn, and did not give in to anything but the thickest smoke. The bullflies (*bolahundarnir*) were even worse, biting monsters about the size of fishflies and appearing about the same time, which drove the livestock mad around midday for six weeks in the middle of summer, so that they found no peace except in the dirt. During this time, the cattle had a very short time for grazing at sunrise and sunset, and no more. This shows the land's quality, the fact that the animals did not become emaciated before summer's end as they endured the insect invasions.

Then there was the fishfly, harmless but irritating, with two hollow hairs or antenna behind them. They hovered in the evenings in great swarms for two or three weeks in summer, settling on men and remaining motionless there, until the clothes were furry in appearance, like a grey pelt. It improved things somewhat when the insect swarms petered out in late summer. Fall and winter were generally the best seasons because then people had time to reflect and plan. If only they could just get rid of the fly, then their settlement would be the most peaceful place in the whole world, and free from all that commotion found elsewhere. Such thinking made its presence quite well known in the area. Therefore, says poet Jón Runólfsson:

> Þetta fólk sem býr á "blettum",
> blóðríkt, kynsælt, fornt í sál,
> eins og sprottið út úr klettum,
> undrast, skelfist tímans mál.

> These folk who farm on plots and patches,
> of purest blood and ancient will,
> raised from distant mountain hatches,
> in fear and wonder prosper still.[22]

In actual fact, it was clear to the settlers that much was lacking in the area and they talked a great deal about all sorts of improvements such as more road construction, the need for railways and savings banks and improvements in agriculture such as larger fields, better livestock breeding and crop production, and so on. Some dreamed still higher, naturally, and turned their gaze out into the wider world. Therefore, says Jón Runólfsson in another verse:

> Þeir helztu ætla' að fara' og fara,
> að fara' að reformera heim;
> en undur smeykur er ég bara,
> að það lognist fram af þeim.

---

[22] Excerpt from Jón Runólfsson's "Landnema rím [The Settler's Rime]," in *Þögul leiftur* (Winnipeg: Sveinn Thorvaldson, 1924). Jón Runólfsson was born in 1856 and died in 1930.

The leaders mean to go and go,
the world to conquer and reform;
My chief concern, I wonder though,
will future leaders be as warm.

But this was easy for Jón to say; his relatives found land south in Minnesota, in the Eastern Settlement, where nothing more was needed than to run the plough through the grassy turf to turn the prairie into the most beautiful fields.

THE BENEFITS OF NEW ICELAND

New Icelanders took this poetry of Jón's as just another joke, but it wasn't all that funny. What he described here was reality. The settlement was a new Iceland; the same problem existed here as back home in that the mindset was far ahead of the practical. This may be proved with few examples.

The issue of religion was much disputed in New Iceland when we arrived there, as it had been since the beginning. At first the disputes were between Rev. Jón Bjarnason and Rev. Páll Þorláksson over the teachings of the Norwegian synod, which Rev. Páll followed. Later, it was over Unitarianism, which Rev. Magnús Skaptason endorsed more and more in those days. The people were divided or fragmented in their beliefs and the Church was in ruin. I am not saying that these circumstances were good, however; progress sometimes goes the wrong way. When men wish to get a little ahead, then they often quarrel over the road to take, and some go astray. It cannot be avoided. Time and trial will make their own judgement in the end. If unity is only bought with a stalemate, then the price is too high.

New Icelanders enjoyed music, just as they do today. Singing groups held practices in Gimli before the turn of the century, as they did north along the Icelandic River and probably elsewhere in the settlement. Young people travelled for miles to go to practices in the cold of winter, often on foot. Those living along the river had a brass band, which was very well rehearsed. Many people learned to play the violin, piano, and other instruments, and this practice increased later. Many New Icelanders have taken exams in various fields of music and have done very well.

Other education wasn't neglected, either. During those first years, my elder brothers became acquainted with other young scholars in New Iceland. Some were beginning their studies at the university level while others were already on that road. In this group were J. Magnús Bjarnason, Jón Kernested, Hjörtur Leó, the Thorvaldson brothers, Sveinn Þorvaldur and Þorbergur, Jóhann Sólmundsson, Jóhannes Eiríksson, and several others. My brother Stefán may be counted among this group. Most of these young men were able to meet together now and then. The entire group had an strong passion for learning in that they didn't study simply to "get ahead." Rather, they took delight in the studying itself. It was clear that this was a characteristic of the baðstofa culture, which I described before. These young men were each from their own corner of the land, so to speak, and they all took delight in talking about all kinds of learning. I am not aware that any of them had their education financed, except perhaps to a very small degree. They worked in the summer to pay for their studies in the winter and often missed two to four weeks of the school year.

It was sometimes said of the Icelandic students that their books took over their lives or consumed them and that they didn't bother at all with the social life as did their other school-fellows. This was a misconception, of course, and arose from a misunderstanding. Most students born in Canada had gone to elementary school for eight years, followed by two or three years in middle school, after which they had four or more years in high school, if they wished to get ahead. Learning can become dry and repetitious for many within a short time and, therefore, fun and games were necessary for these Canadian students, otherwise they would never have survived. But, on the other hand, most Icelanders had had little in the way of public school education during their early years. Therefore, they had to be responsible for educating themselves and it was their pleasure in life to do this. Study was to them what sports were to the others—freedom from the drudgery of daily life—and it was scarcely to be expected that those born in Canada could understand the phenomenon. Living conditions had taught many Icelanders that sport that is called, in this land, "cramming"—devouring a lot of knowledge over a short period of time. There may be many good examples to support this.

Saga's End

When my parents had been in Gimli for three years, a few parcels of land were offered up for sale due to taxes owing. The owners had abandoned them without taking the trouble to offer them up for sale or pay the tax on them. One of these plots was in Húsavík, south of Gimli, the property of Sigurður, the agent. My father bid on the land and got it for eighteen dollars.

Sixteen years before, Björn Gíslason had purchased the property rights to an equally large plot in Minnesota, barely ploughed, for $900, and it was thought to be a good buy. This gives a very good idea of the difference between these two settlements.

Several log cabins were on the Húsavík land, as well as a good-sized blettur. My father built a house on the land in the autumn and moved south there the next spring. My parents lived at Húsavík for the rest of their lives, and we siblings stayed there during the winter months for several years after we got work in the city.

My parents never made a profit in the New World, and therefore could not support us in our studies. Two of us brothers still made it through university, through the means mentioned before.

When Rev. Runólfur Marteinsson took over the ministry in the settlement, my father worked with others to establish or rebuild the Víðines congregation, and my parents belonged to this congregation after that. They lived a peaceful life for what time was left to them, never made a profit, but had enough for their needs. They read the *Decorah Posten*,[23] as well as the Icelandic papers—just as many older folks of our nation did in the New World. They bothered little with politics. However, they gave their neighbours a helping hand whenever it was needed. My mother passed away in the summer of 1904, and my father in January 1919.

I last saw my father when I was on my way to Minnesota, in the summer of 1918. A neighbour of his had recently died, an old man who was rather eccentric. He had been one of those New Icelanders who had been indignant at the religious turmoil. Since he had requested that no clergyman should preside at his funeral, his widow came to my father and asked him to see to the burial. She said that her husband would have gladly agreed to this arrangement. My father agreed to their request. I know that he provided this old man with a good Christian eulogy. He held on to his beliefs, but the disputes and unpleasantness arising from religious matters he let, as Ágúst Vopni puts it, "pass him by."

Men have long ago ceased, to my knowledge, to disparage New Iceland. No one mentions the bolahundar, and múskítan is no longer any worse there than in many other places elsewhere. It has become a spot for enjoyment.

---

[23] A Norwegian-language paper, based in Iowa. (Trans.)

During the emigration years, Rev. Páll Þorláksson said sarcastically that some men up north had now begun to compose odes and patriotic poems about New Iceland as they once had composed poetry about their fatherland. His words were, unintentionally, prophetic. My namesake, the poet Guttormur J. Guttormsson, later composed an excellent ode to the fatherland, the colony. Here are a few lines from this poem:

Bygðin ertu mesta, hin bezta og stærsta,
byggðin ertu helzta, hin elzta og kærsta—
Skógarljóðin hljóma, og óma um engi,
undir leika vogar sem bogar við strengi—

My district is the finest, the biggest and the best,
my district is the eldest, and dearer than the rest.
The forest voices sound, and rebounding echoes sing,
while from inlets music grows, as from bows upon
a string.

Of the two Icelands, the old and the new, one may with truth now say that which Einar Hjörleifsson wrote before of the New World: "You were never lovelier than today."

The children of my parents, ten in all, are as follows:

Jósep Þorsteinn, carpenter, farmer in the Riverton area in New Iceland, married Jóhanna Jónasdóttir Þorsteinsson, from Teigur in Skagafjörður district. She survives her husband.

Þorsteinn, carpenter, organist. Died in Winnipeg; unmarried.

Björg, died in Húsavík in New Iceland; unmarried.

Stefán, surveyor in Winnipeg. Married Ragnhildur, daughter of Gísli Jónsson from Byggðarholt in Lón in East-Skaftafell district.

Oddur, farmer in Húsavík, New Iceland. Married Guðný, daughter of Hermann Gudmundsson from Húnavatn district.

Guttormur, priest in Minneota, Minnesota. Married Rannveig Gísladóttir Egilsson from Skarðsá in Skagafjörður.

Björn, shopkeeper, smith in Winnipeg. Married Helga Kernested, daughter of Jón Kernested, from Meirihlíð in Bolungarvík in Ísafjörður district.

Guðríður, died in Winnipeg as a child.

Guðlaug, married to Skapti, son of Benedikt Arason from Hamar in Laxárdalur. Survives her husband. Lives in Kjalvík in New Iceland.

Einar, farmer at Poplar Park in Manitoba. Married Hólmfríður, daughter of Jónas Jóhannesson from Helgafellsveit in Snæfellsnes district.

—*Translated by Katelin Parson*

JÓN GUTTORMSSON &
PÁLÍNA KETILSDÓTTIR

❖

BY GUTTORMUR J. GUTTORMSSON
POET AT VÍÐIVELLIR NEAR RIVERTON, MANITOBA

*"The pioneer life of my parents could not
be called repetitious or uneventful ..."*

*M*y parents, Pálína Ketilsdóttir from Bakkagerði in East Borgarfjörður and Jón Guttormsson from Arnheiðarstaðir in Fljótsdal, came to America in 1875. They went first to Ontario and stayed in the Gravenhurst area[1] until they moved to Gimli later that year. They stayed there that first brutal winter in New Iceland. The following spring, they moved north to the Riverton area and settled down on my father's homestead, Víðivellir, where they remained to the end of their days. While they lived in Ontario, my father worked laying railroad track and felling trees. Rev. Friðrik Bergmann, then a youth, was the only Icelander he met there. They worked for a time together on the railroad. My father heaped much praise on the boy whenever he remembered him later in life. Meanwhile, my mother worked at various household jobs for

---

[1] Gravenhurst, Ontario, is in the district of Muskoka. (Trans.)

English people while caring for my brother Vigfús, who was then in his first year. During this time, she learned to speak and read English so well that it was quite amazing. This was extremely valuable for her, as those who did not know English were considered to be mute.

After they settled at Víðivellir, they had for a few years, and only over the winter months, a guesthouse called Stopping Place, which was mainly for English travellers. Often, they housed Icelandic travellers, as well, and showed them hospitality but they never accepted any payment from them. Among the welcome guests were English preachers on their way north along Lake Winnipeg to visit their Native congregations. They left behind English papers and books for us, among them the *New Testament* and children's schoolbooks with pictures. My mother read all these with the greatest interest, sometimes to herself, sometimes out loud. I am certain that my brother Vigfús and I have never experienced more enjoyment than when she explained the pictures in these schoolbooks to us. I remember many of the pictures, but will mention only two.

In the first one, a schoolboy is seen leading an old woman who had broken her crutch, fallen, and injured herself. A group of his schoolmates chase them, jeer and scoff at him for "leading this ugly crone," but he pays no attention to them, goes on, and does not part with the old woman until she arrives at the door of her house. In the next picture, the boy is seen riding a beautiful horse and the same group of children walk after him, now serious, full of admiration and awe. It had just so happened that the old woman was a great lady who appreciated and was thankful for the kindness shown to her, and was able to reward it, too. She had sent, as a present to the boy, a horse with a brightly decorated saddle and had sent large gifts to his parents and siblings as well.

My mother was beautiful, with a pale complexion and dark brows and lashes. She was rather fine-boned, neat, and extremely polite and well-mannered. She received a good upbringing, loved to sing, and had a beautiful voice. She read everything she could lay her hands on, both in English and Icelandic. Many people lent her books and papers to read. I remember one issue of *Heimdallur* with a front cover of Nordenskjöld in a fur parka, and also Jón Thoroddsen's collection of poems, which was the first book of poetry that I ever saw, and *Friðþjófssaga* by Esaias Tegnér, translated by Matthías Jochumsson. She knew a great number of poems by heart. We first heard her recite Sigurður Breiðfjörð's poignant poem of the little girl for whom "death came through the door" as well as all the poems from the national celebration in 1874,[2] which she knew the tunes to and often sang. My parents owned mainly books of religious works. I recall the following books: *The Passion Hymns*, a hymnal, *Meditations by Pétur*,[3] *Pétur's Sermons*, Mynster's *Reflections*,[4] *Pétur's Meditational Hymns*, a prayer book, Guðjóhnsen's *First Music-book*, in unison, if I remember correctly, the *New Testament*, Halldór Briem's textbook in English, and the autobiography of Guttormur Vigfússon, member of *Alþingi* [the Icelandic Parliament].[5] *Framfari* had ceased publication before my time, but my parents had collected the issues together and stored them safely away.[6] *Leifur* was later received weekly, and it too was collected. One poem by my mother appeared in *Framfari*, and another in *Leifur*.

---

[2] In 1874 Iceland received its constitution from King Kristian IX.

[3] Pétur Pétursson (1808–1891) was an Icelandic bishop and author of the *Sermons*.

[4] *Reflections on the Principal Points of Christian Faith* by the Danish bishop J.P. Mynster (1755–1854). (Trans.) In 1853 the book was published in Icelandic in Copenhagen: *Hugleiðingar um höfuðatriði kristinnar trúar*, translated by Brynjólfur Pétursson (1810–1851), Jónas Hallgrímsson (1807–1845), and Konráð Gíslason (1808–1891). (Ed.)

[5] Guttormur Vigfússon was Jón Guttormsson's father and Guttormur J. Guttormsson's grandfather. (Trans.)

[6] *Framfari [The Progressive]* was an Icelandic periodical published in Canada from 1877 to 1880. (Trans.)

My mother read aloud extremely well. She read as if she already knew what she was reading in that she could look away from the book and continue reading all the same. I have seen her close the book and go on with the reading right to the end. Musicians call this "reading ahead," and it is something they must learn and be able to do. My mother must have used the same method with words as they do with notes. She could also begin the reading again at the right place without a pause. She read devotions on Sundays, as she sat by the table by the south window, and often looked out that window while she read, without its distracting her. I remember that on winter nights she read stories out of the old *Iðunn, Kvöldvökur* (an extremely entertaining book that is nowhere to be seen here today), *Stories and Adventures* by Torfhildur Hólm, who was then here in the West, and many other books too numerous to count.

My mother's best friends, from when I remember first, were Vilborg from Unaland, mother of Gunnsteinn Eyjólfsson the composer; Kristjana from Brautarhóll, wife of Dínus Jónsson; Sólveig from Bjarkarvellir, wife of Hálfdán Sigmundsson; Sesselja, Gunnsteinn's sister; Guðrún from Fljótsbakki, wife of Lárus Björnsson; Bergrós from Skriðuland, wife of Flóvent Jónsson; Guðbjörg from Espihóll, wife of Einar Einarsson; and Vilborg from Ós, wife of Jón Bergvinsson. The affection and friendship that existed between these women and my mother was exceptional. Many was the Sunday, after devotions, we would row up to Unaland, and there was no place like this that I can remember when it comes to friendship. Guðrún from Fljótsbakki would always come over the river (Fljótsbakki is directly opposite Unaland) for a visit with my mother. Vilborg was bedridden for many years. She was one of the best of all my mother's friends, a singer and well-versed in literature, such an affectionate and good woman and, because of these qualities, she is unforgettable to me. Gunnsteinn was then a youth. He played the *langspil*,[7] concertina, and accordion, and from early on was very interested in singing. There was more to be seen here, by the river, than in many other places. Monotony was unheard of in either summer or winter. In summer there was a steady stream of boats on the river, Aboriginal people's birchbark canoes coming and going, and Aboriginal encampments spread out along the river. A daily crowd could be seen at Möðruvellir, the trading centre, and the sawmill ran all summer. Boats were built and buildings raised and people took leisurely trips down the river in brightly painted boats, complete with songs and accordion music on Sundays.

But my mother considered various things to be major events, which would never have roused the slightest ripples in the souls of others. For example, every summer, we used to hear a bird singing, either while we were at home or out in the forest. No bird could sing as beautifully as this one. This bird did what no other birds did: he sang songs. He knew three tunes and sang each one in turn. Its voice sounded like something between a flute and a piccolo and was so beautiful that it seemed to shine, charm, and enchant. No matter how often or how hard we tried, we could never lay eyes on the bird. Whenever we drew near to the song, the bird would sing from another place, and we never saw him fly. When we saw an especially beautiful and brightly coloured little bird, we thought that this must be the great singer. We found it natural that such a maestro would be so beautifully dressed and it suited him well to be so brilliantly clad. We quickly became aware that these birds were no maestros. I remember that beautiful summer morning as I

---

[7] An Icelandic string instrument. (Trans.)

was putting on my socks, and the door stood open, facing the woodpile in the yard. My mother was outside and I heard this heavenly song coming from the woodpile. My mother rushed into the house, lit up with joy, and said that now she had seen the bird. She described him as very small, dark grey in colour, with white under the chin, which was his one bit of finery. The saying that a king is no one without the clothes didn't apply to him at all. I have since learned that this little bird is known as the Canada bird or white-throated sparrow, and is the only bird in the world that sings tunes corresponding to human rules of art, though these tunes are not composed by men.

What was considered to be another major event in our household was the day when, after the newspaper *Leifur* had just come out in Winnipeg, the editor, Helgi Jónsson, came to visit us. My parents looked up to him and treated him as royalty, and this shows how highly they thought of intellectual life. It should be mentioned how much of a loss the demise of *Framfari* had been to them, but now it appeared that there would be something to take its place.

There was steady traffic during the winter between Winnipeg and Selkirk and various places up north along Lake Winnipeg where fishing and logging occurred. The traffic was mainly along the river by our home. Long rows of colourfully decorated dog teams could be seen carrying pelts down to Stone Fork,[8] which was the trading post of the Hudson's Bay Company between Winnipeg and Selkirk. Up on the collar of every dog was a little pole with a large multicoloured knob on the end, to which was fastened an assortment of coloured silk ribbons, which whirled in the breeze. The back-straps on the harnesses were wide and embroidered with all kinds of decorations made out of glass

---

[8] Likely a misprint of Stone Fort, another name for Lower Fort Garry. (Trans.)

beads and silk. Across the top was a belt of silver bells. The bells made various sounds and were a delight to hear when the dogs were not yelping under the whips of the drivers. The sleds were made out of oak boards, almost a metre in width, called "flat-sleds," with high, brightly painted, curved runners in front and a two-metre-long basket out of burlap, all decorated in bright colours. The Aboriginal people, each with their own team, were always on the move, never wasting time. Most of them wore bead necklaces and silk, rose-patterned, leather jackets. They shouted at the dogs: March! March! cracking their whips, and they could be heard a long way off.

Large horses, two to a sled, were used for transporting fish. The sleds were usually painted a beautiful red and had green shipping crates on them. While the road was still passable, long rows of horse teams were seen constantly by the river. The sleds at this point had not been piled so high with crates that the horses got nowhere! On the side of each horse was a bell made out of gleaming metal that sounded like a church bell. The bells had widely ranging sounds, from broad and narrow, to bright and dim. Depending on how long the horse-trains were, the rhythm grew more varied and beautiful. We stood shivering outside to hear the sound in the distance, which became clearer little by little, and then grew in strength. At around the time that this admirable orchestra was passing by our house, the beat of the instruments had reached its full strength—by then *double forte*—and so continued on with diminishing strength, then dwindled and died out in the distance. The drivers, all in bison-hair coats, sat at the front of the shipping crates and steered their own horses. The crates were full of that enormous, widely acclaimed whitefish, the Lake Winnipeg Jumbo, which is rarely seen nowadays, but was, during those years, so common in those waters that when steamboats ploughed through the shoals of fish, they were cut down in the hundreds by the propeller and floated up to the surface again, head and tail dangling. In those years, the Icelandic River was more travelled than Main Street in Winnipeg, and ferried aid, riches, and spiritual nourishment. When all other roads were impassable, it was passable still. The Icelandic River has been a much-travelled road from time immemorial. It is the reason that contact has been kept and was kept for many hundreds of kilometres in all directions. The river has made a difference. Who can say how many the Icelandic River has saved or how many souls it kept from perishing? Who can say how many souls have withered away out in the empty forest and out on the empty prairies and vanished from this earth because of lack of contact and relations with the outside world?

During the first half of the winter, several groups of men would often go out to Drake's and Rutherford's[9] lumber camps. These men were mostly Scots, likely newcomers to this country, and most of them were fine men, amusing and full of life. There was a lot of fun going on when they stayed with us and had with them a full cask of schnapps. They never went overboard with their fun even though they were drinking. Singing was their main entertainment and it went on long into the night. They sang many excellent Scottish folk songs, as well as an altogether new tune, which seemed to be on every man's lips, "It's one more river to cross."

It once so happened that one of these groups was stormbound for three days with the cask among them and they kept up the festivities all that time. They were "inside," as it was called, in rooms 12 and 14, which they had all to themselves. The first night of this party, we who were "outside" heard an

---

[9] Drake's and Rutherford's in the original, but probably in reference to two separate entities in the area (Brown and Rutherford's and Drake & Co.'s). (Trans.)

extraordinary and appalling sound rise from the din of the party, a discord, one might say, which could not possibly come out of any man's windpipe. The sound was extremely deep and powerful and could be heard at the next farm, so that people began to be curious as to what this might be. A young boy who was then staying with us raced up to the attic and hid himself in bed so as not to hear the noise. After this had taken place, a Scottish gentleman came "outside," obviously the spokesman for the group, and invited us to come "inside" and enjoy the fun with them. The cask now made its way around to my father. We gazed enthralled at a man who stood in the middle of the floor, who readied himself by adjusting a wondrous object that he carried in front of him, under one arm, and on his left shoulder. Various lengths of pipe or pole, with white ivory knobs on the ends and green ribbons that fell down to the floor, stood out from behind his shoulder. He began now his walk across the floor, backwards and forwards, playing Scottish tunes, which were the greatest wonder for us to hear. The bass in particular was extremely powerful. It is worthy of note that I have often seen and heard such instruments since, but never one with such a heavy and powerful bass and I did not think very highly of it because of this. Had the instrument been damaged? This Scottish piper certainly played with artistry and skill. He sweated with the exertion and had to rest himself time and again. Several pranksters in the group then ripped the instrument from him, even shoved him, as if he knew nothing at all. I didn't appreciate at the time that this was in jest. I felt inside just as the farmer who watched the play *Skugga-Sveinn* performed in Seyðisfjörður and, seeing they were about to hang Skugga-Sveinn, leaped up on the stage and announced that no one was going to hang his Sigmund (Long) while he had anything to say about it. At the end of this evening entertainment, the piper came dripping with sweat "outside" to get himself something to drink. He was all smiles and very pleasant. My mother spoke to him and thanked him for the music, and asked what this instrument might be. He said it was called a bagpipe and had cost $500. This was considered to be an enormous sum in those days. The Scottish travellers provided memorable hours of enjoyment for these three nights that they were with us.

The pioneer life of my parents could not be called repetitious or uneventful, as the lives of those immigrants who settled in the deepest parts of the forest and out on the bald prairie, where it was not possible to see the next house and there was no traffic but for wild animals.

My father had little spare time. He worked in the summer at the sawmill from seven in the morning to six at night and then had work on the farm as well. In the evenings after seven, he went out with a hand axe to clear the forest. This left him with no time for reading books or any other intellectual pursuits except on winter evenings. He owned no volumes of the Sagas of Icelanders, but he told us the stories out of many of them so well that he brought the characters to life. The substance of *Grettis saga [Grettir's Saga]*, *Laxdæla saga [Saga of the People of Laxárdalur]*, and *Njáls saga* became thoroughly familiar to us to such an extent that we pretended to be ancient saga heroes and fashioned weapons out of wood for ourselves and battled. Barrel bottoms became shields, our everyday rags turned into sheepskin coats and shirts of mail, and straw hats into gleaming helmets. My father did not own any books of poetry other than the prevalent hymnal and *Meditational Hymns*, but knew many worldly poems and verses, in particular those by Páll Ólafsson and Gísli Víum. A great and heated poetic feud had arisen between them because of a short verse, which Gísli had composed about Páll and a certain Ástríður. My father also knew many songs by heart. He owned a first edition of Guðjóhnsen's hymn book. It was in unison. My father learned some of the tunes in this book from the notes, without any instrument, and he had learned the intervals (to sing from notes) from a man named Jón Reykjalín in eastern Iceland. During those years, I knew only one other Icelander who was as well versed and that was Guttormur Þorsteinsson from Krossavík. My father had learned the parts for various hymns from Jón Reykjalín, which he called "seconds," among them "Blessed Is the Man Who Is Able to Refuse" and "All as the One Bloom."[10] He had us brothers sing the melody, but he sang the lower "seconds." We became extremely taken with the harmony and thought that this was glorious music. He had learned the art of *glíma* [Icelandic wrestling] from Rev. Sigurður Gunnarson, who had competed at the 1874 national celebration in front of Kristjan IX, and my father could bring down any opponent he came up against in glíma. We had fun watching bigger opponents tumble onto their backs, entirely without effort on my father's part. He was extremely fit.

He was a sketch artist with a pencil, although he made little out of it and few people appreciated his talent. I remember two pencil sketches of his. The first was of a horse he had owned in Iceland, the other of a white ox he raised here at Víðivellir. How good the likeness of the horse was, I cannot say, but the drawing of the ox was so accurate that one might have recognized the ox from it. He did not choose the easiest way to draw it, which was to have the picture all in profile. Rather, he had the ox turn its neck and look at the viewer. This required quite a lot of expertise.

---

[10] "Allt eins og blómstrið eina" by Hallgrímur Pétursson (1614–1674). (Trans.)

My father was exceedingly frank and open, gave his opinion without hesitation, and paid no heed to whether it was popular or not. This often landed him in verbal arguments with others, who thought themselves to be similarly unerring, and he then became rather hot-tempered and his eyes shone, and he pounded his fist on the table to underscore his point. I remember that it was not well taken when he let himself be heard at congregational meetings. He was not part of any congregation, but contributed towards a minister and church. The members of the congregation came to him to get contributions and he paid his share of the costs. He had, of course, few friends in the neighbourhood. But the Unaland men were good friends of his, especially Stefán. I never once heard him quarrel with them. They were from the East Fjords, just as he was. It was said that the people from the East Fjords and the people of Skagafjörður got along badly. Those from the east were in the minority here. My father was by nature a very hardy and energetic man, but he also had a sensitive side. When he read or heard the story of Christ's crucifixion, or heard of the misfortunes of someone he knew, he was moved to tears. But he never complained about his own lot in life. He was a hard-working man, but not skilled to the same degree. He was industrious and diligent but did only necessary jobs on Sundays and holidays.

In those years, many fellow Icelanders believed in the existence of ghosts and that several distinguished ghosts had travelled west over the ocean with Icelandic immigrants. People claimed they felt the presence of ghosts and spirits. My father was not superstitious and never sensed the presence of anything unnatural after arriving here. But he said he had once sensed the presence of something in Iceland that no one could explain. It was on the farm Geitagerði in the district of Fljótsdalur. He slept beside the farmer, Ólafur, in an attic room. Wool and various things were stored out in front of the room. Ólafur and my father had gone to bed and spoke together in the darkness late into the night. All at once, there come three heavy knocks on the door. Ólafur is immediately frightened, but my father calls out and asks who is there. This is answered by three knocks, heavier and louder than the first. My father asks again, who is there? Then come three knocks, which fall as if beaten with a "frozen fist," the door and partitioning creaking and groaning so, and it is as if the room shakes with an earthquake. My father then springs out of the bed and calls out that now the guest shall answer for himself, opens the door in a rush with God's word on his lips—"Get behind me, Satan, as it is written"—and so on, as he hunts and rummages through boxes of wool and containers, hurting himself on nails and splinters, so that every finger dripped blood.

He then ran down the stairs, through the passage, and out to the farmyard, without seeing a thing. On the way in and up to the attic again, my father said, he felt a sudden dread that he had not felt before. When my father got into the bed again beside Ólafur, it was as if the farmer had just come up from a swim as he was so covered in sweat that had broken out on him in his fright. My father said that the guest must have had an errand with Ólafur, not him. Those in the district who knew what was going on said this event was connected to a man by the name of Árni Good-Deed. He had fallen out with Ólafur and set out over the countryside towards evening with his guide. They became lost in a snowstorm and died of exposure. Their skeletons were found lying side by side, long after, next to a large boulder.

After he arrived here, my father never sensed any other ghosts or spirits, according to his own account, though there was a well-known ghost den on the neighbouring land to the north of Víðivellir, where there was a large graveyard of Native and Icelandic smallpox victims. It was the homestead of Magnús Hallgrímsson, a former postman from Iceland. He cleared away all the fences and built his house. He wanted to have his farm called Graftarnes [Grave Ness] or Náströnd [Corpse Beach], but neither name caught on. There have been a great number of hauntings there. One old couple, in particular, who had settled on the opposite riverbank, were eyewitnesses to the fact that all was not peace and serenity at the Ness when darkness fell. The old man had only half his sight, unless he looked under the arm of the old woman. But she herself thought that she saw too much, and seized the opportunity, whenever a child was christened in the church, to wash her eyes with the christening water at the end of the ceremony.

One of a few inexplicable phenomena that occurred here at Víðivellir shall now be recounted. My mother and my brother and I—I was four or five years old, my brother four years older—went out to the barn, which was a short walk from the house, to feed the hens and this was a little after noon. We did not stay there long. We had left the house open, but when we came home, the door was locked. A latch was high up on the doorpost, and it had been locked while we were away. My mother tried in vain to open the door. We then went around to the window on the north side of the house. I remember, for I thought it odd, that she pushed with her hands on the panes. At last she got the idea just to open the window and have my brother slip in. The latch was so high up that he had to climb onto a chair to unlock it. After the house had been opened, he did not go in right away, but my mother and I went in. I had an errand in the attic and ran up the stairs but came to a standstill in the hallway and called: "Mama, there's a Native boy up here." The boy, of about the same size as I was then, sat on the floor, to the north of an unused window on the western wall, with his hands clasped in front of his knees. He was motionless, but it seemed to me that he narrowed his eyes at me. I jumped back, ran downstairs again, and, of course, told my mother again, but she did not answer and paid it no heed. I wondered why she was not at all curious about it, but, rather, continued on with her work down below as if nothing had happened. For the rest of the day and on into the evening, I kept vigil by the door, to see whether the boy would go out. The attic window was out of the question, for it was too high up on the house and there were no stairs up to it—no way out of there. I never saw him go out the door.

My father had been working that day, likely at Friðjón's sawmill. When he came home, I told him all that happened, but he did not respond and made out as if it was nothing. I never heard my mother mention one word about it. Still, to this day, I see the boy in my mind sitting by the window and narrowing his flint-black eyes at me. It should be mentioned that I knew of no Native people in the area when this took place. When I told my father of this, he must have thought it was simply nonsense. He had been away and therefore had no opportunity to verify what had happened. But my mother had the opportunity and did not bother with it. What she thought, no one knows. I cannot recall that my mother ever mentioned ghosts or took part in any discussion on the subject. She was not afraid of the dark, but we brothers quickly became so and I still am to this day. We were always eager to hear ghost stories and heard many of them over the years. The truth is that anything to do with horror and the mysterious is enchanting, and, because of this, it is the most powerful element in literature. My father advised us to say our prayers if we became afraid of the powers of night. He said that if we had nightmares or bad dreams at night, it would be because we forgot to say our prayers before we went to sleep or said them without thought or feeling. It was the custom in our household, while my mother lived, that we brothers had to say verses and prayers out loud in the evening, before we went to sleep. I remember where and when our mother taught us the verses and prayers; it was when we were without oil (oil cost seventy cents for the gallon in Friðjón's shop, and had to be used sparingly)! In the darkness, the cookstove was opened. We three sat in front of it and looked into the embers. To be sure, one may make the case that belief in ghosts has its disadvantages, but who can say how great a part it has had in the pious ways and conduct of our nation? If a man did something immensely wrong to his neighbour, what then was more likely or reasonable than that the neighbour would return again to settle the account? Was it not precisely the fear of such visits that ensured that men took such pains to love their neighbour as themselves and do unto others as they would have done unto them?

Every year, our mother celebrated the birthdays of us brothers. Our birthdays were stuck together because they were both in November. She gave us birthday presents and invited some of our friends over "for coffee and chocolate." More than once, Friðjon the merchant, his wife, and daughter Áróra were among the guests. One time, Áróra gave me a tawny horse, on the gallop, which was hitched in front of a wagon, a very remarkable toy. (Áróra became, long afterwards, the wife of Tómas H. Johnson, justice minister for the province of Manitoba.) Once,

I dropped the horse and wagon from the attic down onto the floor below. It was not damaged, but my mother swept it up from the floor and locked it away in a cupboard, said the horse needed to rest itself after that leap. This was intended to teach me to be more careful with the horse.

Guests passing by often visited our home, and that was always enjoyable. My parents were hospitable, good-willed, and helpful. Their house stood open for destitute or poor Icelandic immigrants. Many families have, at one time or another, stayed with us until they were able to find themselves a place elsewhere. I remember that two families at once stayed with us for a full year. Rent or any such payment was, of course, out of the question. This was the common practice in most homes in the area, but it wasn't so among those who had more. The guests who stayed with us were not relatives. Those they knew and yearned to come, either did not come or settled in other Icelandic colonies.

It cannot be said that my mother was happy here. In her mind she was always at home with her parents and siblings. She kept up a constant correspondence with her people. I remember that one summer she had a fixed hope on another of her sisters arriving. I don't know upon what this hope was built, but one morning, when the steamboat *Victoria*, dragging two barges, crept down the river in front of our house, we saw a woman sitting up on the deck on one of the barges with her two children, a boy and a girl. This family fit the description of my mother's sister as the two children were of about the right ages. My mother was so sure that this was the sister she had hoped for, with her two children, that she hurried over to Möðruvellir, where the steamboat landed, to meet them. She came back home again, disappointed, and I have never forgotten that, either.

The situation with my father was a different story. He lived on his hopes for the future and had a "troll's faith"[11] in the country. At the time it did not seem as if there was anything on which to build this faith. When someone showed their amazement that he should settle at this place, which was nothing but an awful jungle and a bog, my father answered happily, "It's a good farm, Víðivellir."

The summer after the big flood, when all hope seemed lost at Víðivellir, he had steady employment in Winnipeg and must have intended to settle down there, for he bought two city lots on Princess Street, which was destined to become one of the most important shopping streets in the city. A receipt for a hundred-dollar down payment was kept for a short while. For these two lots he would have had, a few years later, a sum that would have been sufficient to buy quite a handsome part of the district of Gimli,[12] particularly if he had taken the opportunity of the public auctioning of lands seized for tax, but he had a change of heart and sold the lots later that same summer, at the same price for which he had bought them—and returned again. "Lovely was the hillside,"[13] and a good farm, Víðivellir.

—Translated by Katelin Parson

---

[11] An undying faith, because trolls were noted for their steadfastness. (Trans.)

[12] The district of Gimli was later divided, and the northern part named the district of Bifröst; in the mouths of the locals, variously Beefroast or Bæfrost.

[13] Gunnar of Hlíðarendi's words upon looking towards his farm as he is leaving Iceland after being sentenced to banishment. He chooses to become an outlaw rather than to leave his land. (Trans.)

SIGURBJÖRN JÓHANNSSON & MARÍA JÓNSDÓTTIR

— ❖ —

BY MRS. JAKOBÍNA JOHNSON,
POETESS, SEATTLE, WASHINGTON

"I am very thankful for the example set by my parents and those ten years on the pioneer homestead with them."

 *W*hen my thoughts wander back to bygone times, I find that my memories of my father span a mere thirteen-year period and a little longer for my mother. In January of 1907 I moved away from the first place I had come to love in the New World.

I was in my sixth year the summer that we left Iceland. After arriving in the West, it was as if I first began to become aware of the people and events around me. My father celebrated his fiftieth birthday that winter, December 29, 1889. He died February 9, 1903.

My mother was his second wife and about twenty years younger than he. I was the eldest of four children. Sigurjón, born in Hólmavað in 1886, died right after we arrived in the West. Sigurveig, born in 1890, is a farmer's wife in Argyle, Manitoba.

Egill was born in 1893 and died in 1917, and had settled land in the province of Alberta—he was an intelligent, popular, and hard-working man.

A fair number of individuals from Þingeyri had settled in the district of Argyle. In some instances, kinsfolk and relatives had remained together as a group there, whose numbers were added to by old friends and neighbours from home. There was an atmosphere of trust and friendship between men, and, early on, a thriving social life developed in Argyle. My parents found themselves among friendly and familiar faces from the start. The first autumn and winter, they stayed in the house of my father's brother, who had moved to Argyle from New Iceland with his family. As was the custom, their first home was a log cabin.

When it came time to travel, oxen were hitched to a wagon or sled. My father found these beasts less than amusing, as one is led to believe in a *ferskeytla* [quatrain] from these years:

Minn uxagang nota í veröld ég verð,
en við það ei sálina festi.
Ég létti mér upp, þegar lýkur hér ferð,
um ljósheim á vængjuðum hesti.

Transport and travel my oxen provide,
though hardly a rest for the soul.
My heart will be lighter, at last when I ride,
a winged horse to Heaven, my goal.

The last two lines are inscribed on the gravestone the Argyle settlers raised for him.

In the Argyle settlement, the land was well suited to agriculture. Farming practices advanced rapidly over the course of several years. The population increased, and log cabins grew in size and then vanished altogether to make way for grander dwellings. Horses took over from oxen, and walked easily with machinery over meadow and field—or with a wagon on a road. With the coming of spring in 1890, we moved to the farm of two special friends of my father, who farmed together and were then both unmarried. My mother took on the housework, while my father worked as, among other things, a herdsman for the next two summers. There was, at that time, a fair amount of unsettled grazing land to the south of the main Icelandic settlement, which was put to good use. There were forest-covered hills with a small lake in-between the hills and the countryside was beautiful in the summer. The land here was fertile. The people soon felt at home. They were able to demonstrate their faith in, and loyalty to, the district by celebrating the tenth anniversary of the settlement with a gathering. My father commemorated Argyle in verse as had been the custom in Iceland. Each and every Icelandic colony had its own folk-poet or two. They were most often called upon to recite one of their poems when the people came together.

> Þú skógarhæðum girta grund,
> með gleði skal þess minnast,
> er landar sóttu fyrst þinn fund ... o.s.frv.

> How gladly will your fertile fields
> and forests be remembered;
> my countrymen, when first they came ... etc.

During the third year in Argyle, we moved to the home of another of my father's friends while he did harvest work and other chores for area farmers. But in the spring of 1893, shortly after Egill was born, my parents moved to their own home, on the property of those good friends of my father with whom we had stayed for two years. They owned a large piece of pastureland. My father was able to cultivate a patch of land to grow a vegetable garden on the corner of the slope where the little house was built and to make hay to provide for a few sheep and cattle. I remember him out there with his scythe down in the boggy areas where the big mowing machines could not reach. This was farming on a small scale, but it gave the little household its own sense of being all the same.

We often had visitors and our relationship with friends and neighbours was memorably warm for the ten years we lived there.

One page that I would want least of all to lose from my memory book contains the tale of the all-round helpfulness of the settlers towards each other when the settlement was at its beginning. All the neighbours would come together and "raise the house" if a new immigrant needed help or plough a section of field if someone fell behind, and so on. And no wonder that it was in the spirit of these times that the women came together to form a society among themselves.

Dear pioneers of the Argyle district, heartfelt thanks for all the goodwill so readily shown to my parents during those long-past years!

During the cold winter of 1903, my father suffered a bout of arthritis and was dead within a week. I was teaching school a short distance away, and could, therefore, come home and be with him in his last days. He asked me to read for him, just as he had done in the past. He found comfort and happiness in books to the end of his days, this wise and pure-hearted man who, on life's difficult journey, had lost, to a great extent, his trust in himself but never in the providence of God.

I have many precious memories of these few years in the little house that looked south over the large, grassy fields to the tall forests. In those days I found these trees extremely tall and the forest immense. I have since grown accustomed to another far larger, but perhaps not dearer. For despite various pains that so often closely follow youth, it still has its own enchantments and illusions.

Our house was now no longer on the tranquil corner of the slope. Many years later I was told that flowers had grown there afterwards, which one old neighbour had named "Bína's blooms" and brought home to his garden. Though the gesture may be small, he will be thanked for it when we meet again in heaven.

My mother stayed in the little house while my siblings were growing up under the watchful eye of good friends. She often worked for women in the neighbourhood. My sister married young and my mother lived with her until she died when she was fifty-five years old.

There has been much written on the subject of the hard times in Iceland, which had their own large part in the emigration of so many. I am not going to add to those writings. My parents were poor people, nothing exceptional in those days. My father was past his best years and no longer able to do heavy work. The children were still very young. He had nothing else to hope for than to work a little for others, when it was the busiest during harvest, thereby providing for his family and plot of land.

My parents were role models in the way they lived. This included their principle of never going into debt. My father was the most honourable man imaginable, easygoing, and very careful with his words. Mother was a pleasant woman, energetic and always working. I never saw her idle, certainly, for her energy was boundless for providing for herself and her family. She sewed on the hand machine, spun and knitted everything that the home needed in the way of clothing, and sold a considerable amount of her work in the shops. She could make a great deal out of very little, as she was accustomed to doing from the very beginning. She was able to both prepare food just as it had been made back home and to learn those methods that best suited conditions in the new environment. With her we were always happy. And how beautiful her *laufabrauð* [leaf-bread] was at Christmas! Father showed us children how best to cut it!

If visitors came, coffee was brought to the table and everyone delighted in these times. My father was fun to listen to in conversation, when he had the chance to come into his own. He had the knack of beginning the discussion with everyday chit-chat, and most often drew his topics out from what we were then reading. After Stephan G. Stephansson's poems began to appear, he would sometimes recite the one he considered to be the best and he sometimes had me read a chapter from *Á ferð og flugi [On the Move]*.

After we settled in our own home, I remember how often my mother would sing as she worked. From her I learned both verses and songs "from home"—from her childhood and youth. She had a good memory for such things. She had enjoyed no advantages in any way—far from it. She had seen and tried much and longed to be able to share these things with others. I also know that she was able to do this now and then. I shall never forget how obliging she was, energetic and ready to work. I see, too, in my mind how pretty she was, with such smiling, dark eyes. I remember, too, how sad they became when little Sigurjón died. I think that, at first, she must have hidden deep inside a great yearning for home. She spoke often to me about her mother and brother and certain friends whom she truly loved dearly.

I am very thankful for the example set by my parents and those ten years on the pioneer homestead with them. The Icelandic folk-culture was all around us and was evident in our daily life. The Manitoba winter is sometimes long and hard and the *kvöldvaka* [evening entertainment] at our place was enjoyed just as at home in Iceland. My mother sat with her knitting, the children amused themselves, and Father and I read aloud. He was happy to have me relieve him of the reading, so I became accustomed early on to reading the ancient sagas, *rímur*-poetry [Icelandic ballads], and any other poems and stories that were possible to obtain. As a rule, the people did not own many books, but the settlers had come with something in their trunks all the same. In Argyle, a reading society was established early on, which remedied the shortage, though the requests may have been slow to come during those years. Everyone exchanged books and my father went to great lengths to get us books. The most favoured books were the sagas, which were read winter after winter. I remember what a cause for celebration he thought it when the reading society got a copy of *Flateyjarbók*. I read aloud from it night after night. Father owned *Fóstbræðrasaga [Saga of the Sworn Brothers]*, which we knew nearly cover to cover, as well as *Gull-Þóris saga [Gold-Þorir's Saga]* and the rímur-poetry of Gísli Súrsson.

The first time I was able to buy a book for him, there was no doubt that it should be *Laxdæla saga [Saga of the People of Laxárdalur]* and *Eyrbyggja saga [Saga of the People of Eyri]*, as these he had never owned. But we did own and had learned *Guðrún Ósvífsdóttir*, the epic poem by Brynjólfur of Minna Núpur. With these evening readings at home, I grew to admire the Icelandic language and the nobility and heroic spirit of the Sagas of the Icelanders, which have never lost their hold on my mind. It is also my belief that it is more effective and enjoyable if works of such substance are read *out loud* with feeling and understanding. And that my father did, with his own calm and clear style of reading. I view this as simply the most effective way to teach literature. His facial expressions were likewise charming when he read aloud. We thought the old *Iðunn* to be of value, as well as those few books of poetry then available to us. Then came *Öldin,* with the poems of Stephan G! Of those stories *Öldin* printed, the most memorable to me is "Sögur herlæknisins [Tales of a Field Surgeon]" by Topelius in Matthías Jochumsson's translation. Valtýr's *Eimreið* came later, which was also of interest.

When it drew on towards the kvöldvaka, our mother laid aside her knitting, as Father read God's word. He owned *Pétur's Meditations,* the *Passion Hymns,* an old hymnal, and a prayer book. On Sundays, if we did not go to church, he read from Vídalín's *Sermons* and the appropriate hymn and prayer.

One may ask, perhaps, whether we children always listened to all this reading. The younger ones doubtless amused themselves while they were growing up but I never remember anything other than peace and quiet during the kvöldvaka. At a very young age we all learned to listen during these readings. I recall an incident that Father found amusing, when Egill was a little boy. He said as he was waking one morning that he had dreamt "that Snorri *goði* rode here over the meadow with a party of men, and was in a blue cape." We had undoubtedly been reading *Laxdæla saga* passionately the evening before.

When letters came "from home," usually once a year, we sat and talked of people and events in our valley. My mother's brother seems to have written an exhaustive account of all that was happening. I sat and listened, until I remembered the farm names and felt as if I knew the people who lived on them. When a little time had passed, Father took out a little green-painted writing desk from Iceland and his writing materials. He wrote for a time every day, while we children took care not to disturb him. He took great care with everything that he did. His hand-writing was both even and well formed, so that even though it might only be a letter he was writing, each page actually had a look of beauty, not to mention the look of his poetry.

He told me that he had learned his letters with a feather pen and soot-ink at a blacksmith shop while working for Jón of Einarsstaðir. He had been there for a time when he was ten years old, around 1849. Much has changed in the old country in a century. Educational requirements did not exist then and books were few and far between among the common people. Otherwise, my father was unwilling to bring up the past, least of all in order to speak of his difficulties. He was usually cheerful in conversation, felt at home in Argyle, and was fond of the settle-ment and had friends wherever he went.

I recall that a few of the old men invited him out when he turned sixty. At that time, it was not the custom to do much for the birthdays of older people. But these men had G. Thomas of Winnipeg craft a gold ring, with a harp inlaid in black stone, which they gave to him. It was his first and only piece of jewel-lery, and we had to remind him to put it on whenever he went out on a special occasion. When I myself turned seventy, I had it sized down and wore the ring in memory of my father and the old settlement! And it is held in considerable esteem—perhaps it is not entirely free of the other rings envying it, though they let this be little shown!

How would I describe my father's appearance? He was average in height, well spoken, slightly stooped in the shoulders,

with fine, straight black hair, which scarcely went white at all.
His moustache was dark and his cheeks and chin were always
clean-shaven. He had a high, arched forehead with a bright and
pale complexion. His eyes were grey, quiet, and keen. It is the
calm manner and the gait that I remember so well.

I also remember, when he read eulogies at funerals, how his
very presence reached out to those who were listening. There
were no flowers at funerals in those days, in the little country
church, but it was as if the place was warmed by his sympathy
and sincere faith in the continuation of life.

> ... "Hér er lokið leið,
> og lúinn hvílist,
> fjarri fósturjörð,
> ferða maður...
> Fyrri lét hann líf
> en liðhlaupi færi
> undan drottins
> og dyggðar merkjum."

> ... "The trail ends here,
> and rest for the weary,
> far from my native land,
> a traveller ...
> Sooner would he lose his life
> than fall out of joint
> with the Lord
> and the paths of virtue."

His poem "Vonin um vorið [Hope for Spring]," first printed
in *Öldin,* describes this *inner victory* that my father's life repre-
sents in my mind.

... "En vonin mín um vorið brást mér ekki.
þótt vonabrigði heimsins mörg ég þekki.
Ef frestar það að færa mér sinn varma,
þess fegnari ég tek mér það í arma."
Þú vonin mín um vorið ljóss á hæðum,
mér veitir styrk og logar æðstu gæðum,
Ég á þig frjálsa fleyið mitt ótrauða,
sem fleytir mig í gegn um líf og dauða.

... "Yet the certainty of spring has failed me not,
'though sorry let down often was my lot.
And when its warmth comes tardy to my door,
I welcome its renewal all the more.
You are the promised spring, a light on high,
that lends me strength, and offers me the sky.
My trusty bark on which I freely sail,
through life and death, the voyage will not fail."

GENEALOGY

Sigurbjörn Jóhannsson, born December 29, 1839, at Hólmavað
in South Þingeyjarsýsla, died February 9, 1903, in Manitoba,
Canada. His parents were the couple Jóhann Ásgrímsson
and Rósa Halldórsdóttir, whose family, I was told, came from
Axarfjörður. Ásgrímur, Jóhann's father, was the son of Jón and
lived in Stafn in Reykjadalur, the son of Pétur from Ytrafjall in
Aðaldalur (1703), the son of Helgi of Fjall, the son of Illugi the
priest of Þóroddsstaður, the son of Helgi. Helgi's wife, Pétur's
mother, was Elín Ólafsdóttir, the sister of Arnór of Sandur. From
Helgi and Elín are descended many poets of Þingeyri, as is well
known and widely mentioned.

María Jónsdóttir, born October 22, 1866, at Höskuldsstaðir
in Reykjadal, died in March of 1916 in Manitoba, Canada. Her
parents were the couple Jón Halldórsson and Ingibjörg, daughter

of Erlendur, farmer at Höskuldsstaðir, the son of Eyjólfur, a farmer at Þverá in Laxárdal, the son of Sæmundur. Erlendur's wife was Ragnhildur, daughter of Jón, farmer in Reykjadal. Erlendur's mother and Eyjólfur's first wife was Anna, daughter of Árni Gíslason, district administrative officer and distinguished farmer at Halldórsstaðir in Laxárdalur, and Sigríður, daughter of Sören, farmer at Ljósavatn, the son of Kristján son of Jens, and his wife Guðrún, daughter of Þorvaldur, priest at Hof in Vopnafjörður, the son of Stefán the poet and provost, the son of Ólafur of Vallanes.

—*Translated by Katelin Parson*

EYJÓLFUR JÓNSSON &
SIGURVEIG SIGURÐARDÓTTIR

———— ❖ ————

BY GUÐNI JÚLÍUS OLESON,
FORMER JUSTICE OF THE PEACE
IN GLENBORO, MANITOBA

*"This was our inheritance, which made us devoted
to Icelandic language and literature, and for that
I will never fully be able to thank our parents."*

*M*y parents, Eyjólfur Jónsson and Sigurveig Sigurðardóttir, moved to America from Dalhús in Skriðdalur, Suður Múlasýsla, in 1878 and they went straight to New Iceland, where they first lived at Neðri-Hvammur, a farm by the Willow River just north of Kjarni. During the remainder of their time in New Iceland, they lived for fourteen years at Fagraland, which was a bit farther west and was their legal homestead. Their living conditions were fairly good by the time they decided to make a move to Argyle and this came about because of the following events.

A man named Gottskálk Pálsson had moved to a neighbouring farm in 1887 or 1888. His family was from Þingeyjarsýsla. He named his farm Svalbarði. He was not happy in New Iceland and wanted to seek his fortune elsewhere. In the fall of 1891 he went to work in Argyle as a thresher. The harvest was good in Argyle that year and he returned full of amazing stories about the area's prosperity and had decided to move there the following spring. Gottskálk was an honourable man, entertaining, and a good friend of my father. He urged my father to go with him, and, in the end, he did. My parents moved to Argyle in April of 1892. We lived there for two years and then we moved to Hólabyggð, northeast of Glenboro. My father died there on January 15, 1898. My mother died in the same district on May 6, 1926. There was no land available when we arrived, which was a great disappointment. My father regretted having made this move and he never really recovered from it. Gottskálk moved to Swan River in 1899 and settled there, where he died on October 31, 1919. He is mentioned in the *History of the Swan River Valley 1923*, and also in the *Saga Íslendinga í Vesturheimi* (volume IV, pages 171 and 202).

My father was born on February 21, 1833, at Geitdalur in Skriðdalur. His parents were Jón Guðmundsson and Guðrún Sigmundsdóttir. He grew up in a very poor family and did not receive an education in his youth. He was over twenty when he learned to write while working at small, outlying sheep farms. He had nice handwriting even though he seldom practised it. He worked as a farm labourer for many years in Fljótsdalur, Breiðdalur, and Skriðdalur. He worked the longest, about twenty years, in Fljótsdalur. He also worked with Jón at Víðivellir for many years. He loved Fljótsdalur more than any other district in the world. He was considered to be a hard-working and dependable servant. My father married twice. His first wife was Guðrún Guðmundsdóttir from Geitdalur. She was the sister of Þorvaldur Guðmundsson, who, as far as I know, lived at Geitdalur. Þorvaldur's wife was a remarkable woman and was bestowed with the most beautiful name that exists, Svanhvít. Guðrún died in Iceland. Three of their children grew to adulthood and moved to America with my father. Guðmundur was born September 7, 1866, and died in Winnipeg on July 1, 1945. Guðbjörg was born November 15, 1870, and died in Blaine, Washington, on January 23, 1908. Svanhvít was born March 11, 1873, and died in September of 1894. Guðmundur was a talented carpenter and worked in that trade all his life. He was also a good marksman. His wife was Gíslína Gísladóttir from Hóll in Kaldakinn. She is still alive. They had six children, all still living. Theirs is a large and beautiful family. Guðbjörg married Árni J. Paulson from Kambastaðir in Ljósavatnsskarð. She died, as is recorded here before, at a young age. Their three children are all living.

My father's second wife, my mother, was Sigurveig Sigurðardóttir and she was born at Breiðamýri in Vopnafjörður on August 9, 1844. She had been my father's housekeeper in Iceland and came with him to America. Jón Bjarnason married them during their first years in New Iceland. My mother's parents were Sigurður Rustikusson and Sólveig Sigurðardóttir. They came from families of great integrity from the east coast of Iceland, tracing their genealogy back to ancient times. My mother began to work at an early age at various places in Vopnafjörður and in Jökuldalur. She worked for a long time at Hof for the archdeacon, Rev. Halldór Jónsson, whom she held in higher esteem than any other man. He was a politician and a minister and was renowned nationwide. She often mentioned, with deep respect, Halldór and her stay at Hof.

My parents were middle-aged when they moved to America. My father had tried to get a homestead in Fljótsdalur, the district he loved most of all, but it never came to be. The story goes that men were afraid that he would become a dependent of the state and therefore he moved to Canada. He did not have much left over after he had paid for the travelling expenses. Many other people had to deal with the same problem.

New Iceland was three years old when my parents settled there. They came too late for the government grant and considered it fortunate, as they had escaped the misery of the smallpox epidemic. They arrived to begin a new battle: they were penniless, homeless, and did not speak any English. They were not totally destitute, however, because a good friend of my father's, Jón Jónsson from Gilsárstekkur, who lived at Laufás, helped them, which they greatly appreciated. He welcomed them again with the same graciousness when they moved to Argyle in 1892. We had just arrived there when a terrible snowstorm hit late in April and it was one of the worst spring storms ever. The first years were difficult for them. As soon as they were able to, they built on their legal homestead, Fagraland. The trees in the forest were sky-high, there were no roads, and the mud was so terrible that it was almost impossible to travel around the farm, especially when it rained. The flies were unbearable in the summer heat and both the mosquitoes and black flies pestered the animals so badly that men had to build fires to smoke them out night and day. People tried to protect their houses against the vermin by using finely woven nets. My father built a nice log house with a timber roof. He used wood shavings to waterproof the roof. My parents struggled to have enough money for clothes and food because their income was meagre. I have often marvelled at my mother's ability to make do with what she had on hand. It was nothing short of a miracle. The same could be said about many of the other women settlers as well, since the heaviest burden usually fell upon them. My parents tried to establish a herd of cattle and sheep as soon as possible. As could be expected, it was slow going. The milking cow was a lifesaver for the settlers and it remains as such to this day. It often made the difference between life and death to have this supply of food all year around. Going to the barn with my mother to milk the cow in the evening is one of my first memories. In Iceland it was not a custom for men to milk cows and that custom continued here throughout the years. My mother was intelligent, well read, and outgoing. She knew many poems and ballads by heart and I still remember some of what she taught me in my youth. She taught me to read and write, by using both the Bible and *Heimskringla*. I was told that I was quick to learn to read. Nevertheless, my sister Guðrún was ahead of me in such matters. My mother loved to travel but the only long journey she made in this country was to visit her relatives in Minnesota and Dakota in 1897. She went south with the people going to the ecclesiastical council assembly and stayed for a month. She often went to visit her friends within the district, especially in later years. Once she walked to visit Karvel Halldórsson and his wife Sigrún, and I went along. At the time, I was six or seven years old.

My father was eleven years older than my mother. He was already physically worn out when he arrived in this country. He had a double hernia and was unable to work much the last few years but he was a strong man and did not go easy on himself. Like many, he had worked like a slave in Iceland for little pay and physically that took its toll on him. I was devoted to him and loved him very much, for he was a good father to me. I followed him whenever I could; I went with him out into the woods and he often carried me on his back. Once I was with him out in the woods and we came to a bog where a haystack stood. He set fire to the dry grass around the haystack and intended to burn around it so as to keep it safe from the forest fires that were burning in the area at that time. Somehow he lost control of the fire and the haystack burned to ashes. He asked me not to tell anybody about this misfortune, which I promised to do, and I kept my promise. Later on, he spoke of the incident and I was praised for my discretion.

The quality of life during the early pioneer years, as could be expected, was not very good. There were many daunting obstacles to overcome. That is, of course, a common story among settlers anywhere in the world. The first chore was to build a shelter for the family and the animals that the settlers had managed to acquire. Next, provisions were needed for the farm. My father was able to gather a few cattle, sheep, and chickens. We managed during the first years by living on milk, potatoes that we were soon growing, and fish, which my father caught from the lake and carried home over many kilometres. Flour, coffee, sugar, and other necessities that had to be bought from the store were often not available because gold and silver were scarce. There were no luxuries to speak of and I never noticed that my father ever had any alcoholic drinks on hand. I only saw him tipsy once when he came home from town, and I never knew him to use tobacco. He never failed to bring us a little bit of candy or other sweets when he came home from a shopping trip. Those occasions were wonderful. When he had the opportunity, he went to Winnipeg to work for short periods to get some money to buy necessary supplies. After my older siblings had moved to Winnipeg and found work, they were able to help to some extent. My brother Guðmundur sometimes went hunting for animals and birds to eat and my father snared rabbits. We thought that there was nothing better than a meal of rabbit. My brother Kristján and I also had success hunting rabbits this way when we got older.

During the first years there were no vehicles for transportation and people had to walk everywhere. This took a long time and was tiring. After the first few years, my father acquired an ox and a sled. I remember the ox well. He was a beautiful animal of good quality and his name was Bob. My father went on shopping trips to Winnipeg at least once or twice during the winters after he acquired the ox and this was great progress. When he went away on errands, my mother was left alone to look after the farm and the children, but sometimes they got someone to stay with her. The pioneer women showed great courage by staying alone in these great empty lands while their men were working or away on some other errands. The women feared the Native people because, in Iceland, it was preached that they were dangerous. This was done in order to frighten people into staying in Iceland instead of moving to America. It gave many pioneers a scare when the Native rebellion took place in Saskatchewan in 1885. Even though the women were afraid, they did not let it affect them. During the time that the Icelanders were settling in Canada, the Native people were in the forests, on the plains, and on uninhabited lands. They were often hungry and fared badly, but they never showed any ill will toward the settlers. Rather, the opposite. Still, it is no wonder that women who were home alone with their children were afraid of them because of the many stories they had heard. The Icelandic pioneer women had to be brave. Native people often visited us but they were all polite and courteous. My father usually offered them food and they ate heartily. It was obvious that they were hungry. I especially remember one man who had come a few times and he liked to get a piece of bread or some other food. There was no conversation between him and my father because neither could understand the other, except through the universal language of friendship.

It happened quite a few times that my parents helped recent arrivals from Iceland. I remember some of these people well. It was done out of goodwill and the desire to help others. My parents wanted to help those who were hard-pressed and they shared what they had. Often I heard my mother recite this verse:

Hvar þú finnur fátækan á fornum vegi,
gjörðu 'onum gott, en grættu hann eigi,
guð mun launa á efsta degi.

Where you find the less-favoured along life's way,
lend them a hand, do not turn them away,
God will reward on your final day.

This came from her heart and she lived according to her beliefs, helped those in need, and supported good causes as much as she was able.

We grew up in an Icelandic environment that was no less Icelandic than back at home on the farms in Iceland. Therefore, the morals and customs of the settlers were the same as they were accustomed to in their native land, and they intended to preserve them here. I remember the sermons that were read and psalms that were sung in the evenings as well as the Sunday sermons of Dr. Pétur. After the reading, everyone wished each other well with a kiss. Otherwise, in the evenings during the winter, we read stories, ballads, sometimes poetry, and also *Heimskringla*, which was the only newspaper that came to our home. My father bought it from the beginning. As my sister Guðrún and I grew older, it became our task to read. My parents valued books and knowledge, as has been mentioned here before, but they had little education except for what they were able to acquire on their own as adults, which was mostly reading, writing, and a little bit of mathematics. My mother's eyesight was poor from an early age and she blamed it on the fact that she had read quite a bit by the light of the moon because there was no other light to be had. The Sagas of the Icelanders, the ancient Nordic history, the history of the kings of Norway, and ballads and poetry of the nineteenth century were held in high esteem, as were Icelandic proverbs and aphorisms. My mother knew many poems by heart and my father knew many ballads. He often recited the ballads aloud, which we found entertaining. Mother and Father would be sitting down, doing some kind of work during the reading, which was an old Icelandic custom. After the book had been read, it was discussed at length. I remember how captivated we were when *Njáls saga* was read. Many things came up during our discussion of it. My parents' favourite ballad poet was Sigurður Breiðfjörð. My mother loved the ballad about Bernótus the most while my father was very fond of the ballad of Úlfar.

I want to mention people whom I remember who lived in our area in Víðinesbyggð from 1886 to 1902: Kristján Kernested and his wife Sigríður at Kjarni; Þorsteinn Sigfússon at Efri- Hvammur—his wife Anna was a midwife; Elías Kernested and his wife Ólöf at Laufás; Benedikt Arason and his wife Sigurveig at Kjalvík; Jón Abrahamsson and his wife Anna from Húsavík; Albert Þiðriksson and his wife Elín at Steinsstaðir; Sveinn Kristjánsson at Framnes and his wife Veronika Ragnheiður; Sturlaugur Felsted and his wife Soffía at Hólmur; Þorsteinn Mjófjörð and his wife Ingibjörg also lived at Hólmur— Þorsteinn was Ingibjörg's second husband; Þorvaldur Sveinsson and his wife Halldóra at Steinkirkja; Friðfinnur Þorkelsson and his wife Þuríður at Skógar; Björn Jónsson and his wife Guðný at Sviðningur; Gottskálk Pálsson and his wife Þóra at Svalbarði (Þóra and Björn at Sviðningur were siblings; their half-brother was Valdimar Ásmundsson, who was the founder and editor of the periodical *Fjallkonan*); Jóhann Schaldemose and his wife Kristín at Neðri-Hvammur; Magnús Jónsson from Fjall and his wife Margrét at Hjarðarholt; Þorbergur Jónsson and his wife Guðbjörg at Viðvík; Þórarinn Jónsson and his wife Sigríður at Reykhólar; Þórarinn, Þorbergur, and Magnús from Fjall were brothers. Þórarinn drowned in Lake Winnipeg in the fall of 1890 along with Þorsteinn Ásgrímsson, who was then newly married to Sigríður, a sister to Guðbjörg, the wife of Þorbergur (Þórarinn was a farming specialist from Iceland and a handsome man). A man by the name of Baldvin lived at Ljótstaðir, but I don't know his last name. His wife's name was Jórunn. They were seniors. Jórunn died during the latter part of this period and hers was the first and only funeral that I went to in New Iceland. Páll Gunnlögsson and his wife Nanna lived at Sunnuhvoll (they were a handsome pair, intelligent and talented poets). Bjarni Pálmason and his wife Anna Eiríksdóttir lived first at Bjarnastaðir and later at Víðirás until their death.

In 1887 Ísleifur Ísleifsson and his wife Þorbjörg Þorsteinsdóttir moved from Húnavatnssýsla with their three boys. The first winter they lived a few kilometres south of Gimli. The woman and two of the boys caught typhoid fever and were placed under quarantine. Ísleifur was now in trouble. His wife and two boys were sick and the youngest boy was only one year old and everyone was afraid of the typhoid fever. My mother had heard of his circumstances and it so happened that one day she was walking in the northern part of the district and came to the crossroads, south to Kjalvík and west to Kjarni and Fagraland. She saw a stranger walking along the road so she stopped and waited, greeted him, and asked him for any news. She then told him she had heard about his situation and asked how things were going. He told her everything. She suggested that if he had a small sled that could be easily pulled, he should get the little boy ready, put him on the sled, and bring it to this same place at a given time the next day. She would be there to meet him and would look after the boy until the sickness had passed. Ísleifur reminded her that this sickness was contagious and could be dangerous. She said she would manage. Ísleifur brought the boy and he stayed with us the whole winter without incident. The boy's name was Þorsteinn Albert and he now lives in Winnipeg. My mother and Þorbjörg became friends for life.

I remember well those pioneer days and the poverty, but also the good times we enjoyed, as if one appreciated life and its value more than one does now in times of plenty. There are many memories that clearly stand out in my mind but perhaps the most memorable one is the last Christmas while my father was still alive, in the year 1897. Christmas and Easter were the brightest stars for us during the year, celebrations we always looked forward to because then—even if there wasn't much to flaunt—we made a show of what we had. Those days were the highlights of the year, different from all others. First came the Christmas reading, then the precious little gifts, followed by the festive meal, more glorious and much better than we had everyday. We played and talked until it was very late and the Christmas candle burned all night. Thankful for a happy Christmas, we went to bed and slept the sleep of the righteous until morning. When the Christmas season was finished, it was back to the everyday routine.

On Monday morning, January 3, 1898, my father went out to the hills about two miles away to get dry firewood and I went along. Just as we arrived home, my brother Kristján came along with an Icelandic farmer who wanted me to come and stay with him for a while and so I left with him. On January 10, my father went to Glenboro and, on his way home, he came by the farm where I was staying. That was the last time I saw him in good health. That same night on his way home, as he was trying to catch the horses that had run away from him, he suddenly became ill. It was with great effort that he finally caught them. A doctor from Glenboro came to see him and said that Father had acute pneumonia. He did seem to improve as time passed and we thought he was over the worst, but in the evening twilight of Saturday, January 15, he passed away; it was as if a light had been extinguished. That was the first time I saw a man die and it was a shock for me and all of us. We mourned him greatly. With God, one can not quarrel.

My parents were always ready to recite Icelandic verses and poetry, as well as proverbs and aphorisms, which they did at any given opportunity. This was our inheritance, which made us devoted to the Icelandic language and literature, and for that I will never fully be able to thank our parents. Language is the key to treasures that are worth more than gold. Here are a few samples of aphorisms and proverbs, which I learned in my youth at home.

Morgunstund gefur gull í mund. [Morning so grand gives gold in hand.]

I heard my mother sometimes say this when a man she didn't like was being discussed and praised: *Já, hann er sjálfsagt góður og gjafalítill.* [Yes, he is doubtless fine, and ill-refined.]

Auðþekktur er úlfur í röð. [Obvious is the wolf in sheep's clothing.]

Hvað ungur nemur, gamall temur. [Lessons learned in youth last a lifetime.]

Uxinn fór til Englands og kom aftur naut. [The ox went to England and returned as a steer.]

Á misjöfnu þrífast börnin best. [Adversity builds character.]

Á flótta er fall verst. [The fall while in flight is the worst.]

Ungur má, en gamall skal. [Youth may, but the aged must.]

Allir dagar eiga kvöld um síðir. [The darkest day will run its course.]

Svo bregðast krosstré sem önnur tré. [A cross, like other timber, falls in time.]

Sá sem árla fer að hátta, og árla upp rís, auðmaður verður, hraustur og vís. [Early to bed, early to rise, makes a man wealthy, healthy, and wise.]

Þeim er mein sem í myrkur rata. [Those who make their way in darkness are at peril.]

Margt kemur upp þega hjúin deila. [Many things surface when couples quarrel.]

Frændur eru frændum verstir. [A kinsman is most cruel to his own.]

Ekki eru allar ástir í andliti fólgnar. [Love also lies beneath the surface.]

Gott er að hafa barn til blóra og kenna því alla klækina. [It's good to have a child as scapegoat, and place on him the blame for pranks and tricks.]

Fáir neita fyrstu bón. [Few refuse the first request.]

Ef þú vilt erindi þínu framgang, þá farðu sjálfur, ef þér er sama, þá sendu annan. [If your errand is important, go yourself; if indifferent, send another.]

Betra er hjá sjálfum sér að taka en sinn bróður að biðja. [It's better to make do with what you have than to beg from your brother.]

Betur sjá augu en auga. [Greater insight has the group than the individual.]

Einu auganu er hætt, nema vel fari. [One eye is vulnerable, unless things go well.]

Blindur er bóklaus maður. [A man without books is blind.]

Betri er húsbruni en hvalreki, á fyrstu ári. [Better a burned house than a beached whale in the first year.]

Betra er að veifa raungu tré en aungvu. [It's better to shake the wrong tree than no tree.]

Margan átti ég alvininn / úlf í klæðum sauða / en hálfkunningi mætur minn / mér var trúr til dauða. [Many a true and trusted friend, / tested come out wanting. / While devotees more distant send, / devotion true, undaunting.]

Auminginn sem ekkert á / einatt kinn má væta / sæll er sá sem sjálfur má / sína nauðsyn bæta. [The vagrant living on the street, / tears alone can muster. / Happy is he with means to mete, / and dole his own life lustre.]

These are just a few examples and I'll stop here. Aphorisms and proverbs have always been favourites of mine and a part of my "daily bread" during my life. Poetry is something else that has given strength to the common Icelander for a thousand years. It had been said that the following verse was written for my father by a woman in Iceland when he left for America. I am not certain whether it is true but the verse deserves to live on:

Hverfi frá þér hryggð og pín
hvar sem dvelst í heimi
bæði þig og börnin þín—
blíður Drottin geymi.

Fare you well and free from grief,
far on life's broad highway.
May God your children grant relief,
and keep you on his byway.

My parents had five children. They have all died except the one who writes this. 1) Sigurbjörn died at an early age, during the first years in New Iceland. 2) Guðrún Stefanía Paulson was born March 22, 1880, and died June 10, 1952. 3) Guðni Júlíus (I myself) was born May 22, 1882. 4) Kristján Aðaljón was born June 3, 1884, and died March 22, 1937. 5) Halldór Tryggvi was born September 7, 1888, and died July 7, 1911. My mother was very old. She died May 6, 1926.

We all lived near one another until 1911. After that, my mother lived most of the time with my sister Guðrún and I think she enjoyed her old age. Her health and memory were good until the end. She knitted and spun and by nature she was hard-working and tidy. She loved to visit with her friends. She had many loyal ones whom she visited regularly for days at a time. I am grateful to her friends for their part in making her last days brighter and happier. The obstacles that the pioneers had to face were difficult, and she, as so many others, deserved to rest in her old age. My mother was not bedridden and she died of natural causes when the time came. She said her goodbyes and was not worried about the night or the coming day. Her siblings were: 1) S.S. Hofteig; 2) Stefanía Johnson in Minnesota; 3) Hólmfríður Johnson in Watertown, South Dakota, and later Portland, Oregon; 4) Daníel Sigurðsson, the postman for the east and south parts of Iceland. He lived at Steinstaðir in Skagafjörður, and came to America in 1914, staying for one year; 5) Björn S. Heiðmann, who lived close to Glenboro, Manitoba; and 6) Kristján, who was a farmer in Austfirðir and did not come to America. All of them lived to a very old age and have since passed on.

My father was about six feet tall and fairly broad-shouldered, a strong man, a hard worker, and skillful. No doubt, he died before his time from working too hard, both here and in Iceland. He had neither power nor money. I often heard him recite this verse:

"Fátæktin var mín fylgikona
frá því ég kom í þennan heim."

"Famine was my fellow man,
from thence I came into this world."

Despite the hardship, I seldom heard them complain. They were hospitable, as was customary in Iceland. They were united in their effort to stay out of debt (that is a virtue). When my father died, he was a debt-free man.

—*Translated by Árný Hjaltadóttir*

THE CONTRIBUTORS

Sigurlína Backman (née Johnson) was born in 1896 in Saskatchewan. When she was six years old, she moved with her family to Langruth, Manitoba, where she later became a schooteacher. She married Dr. Kristján Jens Backman of Lundar, who was a general practitioner at Eriksdale and, later, a specialist in Winnipeg before he was appointed Director of the Division of Venereal Disease Control in the Manitoba Department of Health. Sigurlína (Lee) died in 1985.

Rósa Benediktsson (née Stephansson) was born in 1900 in Markerville, Alberta, where she grew up. In 1919, she left her parents' home (which later became an historic site, the Stephansson House) to study home economics at the Alberta School of Agriculture in Olds for two years. She married Sigurður Benediktsson and they farmed in Alberta. Rósa was instrumental in the restoration of her parents' homestead. In 1976, it was designated a Provincial Historic Site, and, in 1982, the Stephansson House was opened to the public. Rósa was also a key player in the process of having Stephansson's poems translated into English. She died in 1995.

Valdimar Björnsson was born in 1906 in Minneota, Minnesota, where he grew up. While receiving his education at the

University of Minneapolis, he worked simultaneously at his father's printing press in Minneota. He served in the navy during the second World War. He married Guðrún Jónsdóttir. After moving to St. Paul, he became an editor for the St. Paul Dispatches and Pioneer Press. In 1950, he was elected State Treasurer and served until 1966. In his retirement, he moved to Minneapolis, where he was named Consul of Iceland. He died in 1987.

Guttormur Guttormsson was born in 1880 at Krossavík in Vopnafjörður, and emigrated with his parents from Iceland to New Iceland, Manitoba, in 1893. He was educated at Wesley College (Winnipeg) and Maywood Seminary (Chicago). Ordained by the Icelandic Evangelical Lutheran Synod in 1909, he served as the synod's home missionary for three years. From 1912 until 1918, he was parish minister at the Concordia Lutheran Congregation in Churchbridge, Saskatchewan, concurrently serving the nearby Logberg Lutheran Congregation. From 1918 until his death in 1956, he served St. Paul's Lutheran Church in Minneota, Minnesota, concurrently serving the Vesturheim and Lincoln congregations. Guttormur was co-editor of *Sameiningin* from 1914 until 1943.

Guttormur J. Guttormsson was born in 1878 at Víðivellir in Riverton, Manitoba. A gifted poet and a farmer, he was (apart from attending three years of primary school) a self-taught man. He took on various jobs until he settled down as a farmer at the place of his birth, Víðivellir, in full view of the Íslendingafljót, the river that, at the time of Guttormur's childhood, was livelier with traffic than Main Street in Winnipeg. His wife was Jensína Daníelsdóttir. One of the leading Icelandic poets in the New World, and, like Stephan G. Stephansson, a revolutionary spirit, Guttormur is the author of several collections of poetry. One of his best known poems is "Sandy Bar," published in 1920 in *Bóndadóttir (Farmer's Daughter)*. He also wrote plays and published numerous pieces in newspapers and periodicals. A great lover of music, too, he played in a brass band. He died in 1966.

Jakobína Johnson (née Sigurbjörnsdóttir) was born in Iceland in 1883 in Suður Þingeyjarsýsla, and moved with her parents to Canada in 1889, settling in the Argyle district near Winnipeg. A gifted poet, translator, and a literary scholar, she was educated as a teacher in Manitoba where she worked until she moved, with her husband Isak Johnson, to Victoria, BC, and from there to Seattle. An award-winning cultural bridge builder between the Old and the New World, Jakobína's books of poetry (like *Kertaljós* from 1939) were published in Iceland. Her translations of Icelandic and Icelandic-Canadian literature are renowned, handing down to future generations unique, poetic voices such as that of Stephan G. Stephansson and Icelandic playwright Jóhann Sigurjónsson. Jakobína died in 1977.

Guðni Júlíus Oleson was born in Manitoba in 1882. He grew up in the Víðinesbyggð until he moved with his parents to Argyle in 1892. A couple of years later, the family moved to Glenboro, where he later became a judge. He also served as a chairman of the board of the Glenboro Lutheran Church and superintendent of its Sunday school. He was also president of the Glenboro Board of Trade and was involved in local politics. His widow, Gudrun Kristin Oleson, died in 1969 at the age of ninety-two. Guðni died in 1957.

A NOTE ON THE TRANSLATORS

*T*here are four translators at work in this collection. Nina Campbell translated the essay on Stephan G. Stephansson and Helga Jónsdóttir, written by their daughter, Rósa Benediktsson, previously published in Joanne White's *Stephan's Daughter: The Story of Rósa Siglaug Benediktsson.* I would like to thank Nina Campbell and Joanne White for permission to republish the piece. Árný Hjaltadóttir and Katelin Parson translated the other six essays, three each. The former graduated in 2006 from the Department of Icelandic Literature and Language with an MA degree, specializing in Translation Studies and the translation of Icelandic–Canadian literature. The latter is also a former student of the department, currently studying at the University of Iceland for a Master's degree in translation studies. David Gislason, a poet, translator, and farmer in the New Iceland area, translated the poetry, proverbs, and the aphorisms in all six essays.

Pat Odegard, an MA student in the department, who also aspires to Translation Studies, edited the translations along with myself. It should also be noted that Kristin Sumner, a poet and Pre-Master's student in the department, proofread the translations. In fact, the project was viewed from the beginning as a valuable opportunity for graduate students at the Department of Icelandic Language and Literature to take on a challenging and creative assignment. David Gislason's translation of the poetry, proverbs, and the aphorisms can also be viewed as a living example of the way in which the Icelandic language and cultural heritage continue to survive in North America. Needless to say, any shortcomings in the translations are my responsibility.

—*Birna Bjarnadóttir*